A Sloan Product

A Memoir of a Lost Boy

Neil L. Selinger

Published by World Audience, Inc.
(www.worldaudience.org)
303 Park Avenue South, Suite 1440
New York, NY 10010-3657
Phone (646) 620-7406; Fax (646) 620-7406
info@worldaudience.org

ISBN 978-1-935444-71-8
©2011, Neil L. Selinger

To the other three goonks who survived it all with me.

And to Rima who has made it all worthwhile.

February 16, 1984, 2107 Albemarle Terrace, Brooklyn, New York

The small kitchen, with its exposed brick wall and second-hand dinette table, is the only room that still feels like mine. The house now belongs, mostly, to my ex-wife, the final item we had to divvy up, just as we had with the books and records. The kitchen cabinets and wood trim are splotched and streaked, a remnant of our first home improvement project. Shortly after we moved in, we went to Sears and bought a heat gun and some paint scrapers. The plan was to strip the layers of old paint off of the wooden cabinets and door frames, restoring them to their original patina. We worked at it for a few weeks before we ran out of steam, one more entry in the long list of things never completed.

I am here in Brooklyn for a few days, caring for my three year-old daughter while Judy is off in Martha's Vineyard at some romantic inn with her current lover. For some reason, after I put Hannah to bed I decide to sit at our old kitchen table. I am staring at my unfinished handiwork when the phone rings.

"Hi, Honey," my mother says. "How is Hannah?"

"She's fine. How did you track me down?"

"I called your apartment. One of your roommates told me where you were. Honey, I have some bad news. Dad died tonight."

It is the call I have been expecting for the last twelve years, ever since my father had a massive heart attack when I was a freshman in college.

"No. What happened, Mom?" I try to maintain my composure as I speak, but I fear I overdid it. My words sound flat.

"They said it was congestive heart failure. He collapsed in the bedroom. By the time the ambulance got him to Bayshore Hospital he was gone."

My mother is her usual self, her cool affect masking any emotion. But I can hear my grandmother, my mother's mother, carrying on in the background. As histrionics are her specialty, no doubt she will turn my father's death into her latest personal tragedy.

"Let me make some plans for someone to stay with Hannah. I'll be out first thing in the morning. I'll help you make all the arrangements."

I sit with my head in my hands, but I will not cry. I had cried plenty when he had his first heart attack, and cried some more during his subsequent hospital stays. But at this moment I am numb. And angry. Lately, I am angry most of the time. Here I am, thirty years old, my marriage over, renting a small bedroom in an apartment with two roommates I barely know, then this week sleeping alone in my old house with my toddler so Judy can go off with her latest. And now my father is dead at sixty-two.

Part I

Where I Come From

Chapter One

I was born with a plastic spoon in my mouth and a paper cup in my hand. At least that is how it seemed growing up at Sloan Products, the wholesale paper and toy business run by my maternal grandmother Olga Sloan and the rest of my extended family in the small town of Matawan, New Jersey. For much of my childhood, before deaths and the custody battle started to trim our ranks, thirteen members of my family (great-grandmother, grandmother, two great-aunts, great-uncle, parents, aunt and uncle, brother, two cousins, and me) lived and worked together, our own self-contained shtetl in central New Jersey. We ate our meals utilizing the paper plates and napkins, plastic cutlery, and Lily-Tulip paper cups that were the foundation of the family business. To this day, I eschew disposable dinnerware whenever possible.

My memories of those years are dominated by the oversized presence of my grandmother, and especially the feud between her and her younger brother, my great-uncle Charlie, and the effect it had on my parents. It seemed as if Olga and Charlie battled twenty-four hours a day, seven days a week, and the other adults in the household spent much of their time and energy trying to diffuse the war that enveloped them. As a child, I sought solace from the constant bickering and chaos by retreating to my room and reading. First, it was comic books, followed by book series for young boys, such as *Chip Hilton, All-American, The Hardy Boys*, and *Tom Swift*. Then in the fifth grade, I methodically read the entire World Book Encyclopedia, a background that came in useful during the Trivial Pursuit battles of the 1980's. As a teen, I read the entire works of Updike, Roth, Vonnegut, and Heller, while also working through large portions of Shakespeare, Joyce, Twain, Faulkner, and Hemingway. When

I was not reading, I was often lost in my own little world, a chronic daydreamer. During those years, I worked at Sloan Products after school and over the summer, as did my brother and cousins. Mostly, I carefully observed the peculiarities and odd inter-relationships of my older relatives. I vowed to hightail it out of Matawan at the first opportunity. I did, but hardly a day goes by without my thinking about growing up in the world of Sloan Products and the far-reaching impact that those years had on me well into adulthood.

I also imagine what it would have been like if we had all taken the time to tell each other how we really felt. In this fantasy, I envision a scene something like this from a play that exists only in my head, a play I call "The Way We Were Not":

Scene: Sloan/Ungar/Selinger family Thanksgiving 1965, in the large dining room of 59 Freneau Avenue, Matawan, New Jersey

Cast:　　*Neil, age 12*

　　　　Olga, his grandmother

　　　　Helen, his mother

　　　　Jules, his father

　　　　Howie, his brother, age 14

　　　　Sandi, his cousin, age 15

　　　　Eddie, his cousin, age 11

　　　　Charlie, his great-uncle

　　　　Sadie, his great-aunt

　　　　Annie, his great-aunt

　　　　Taffy, the family Poodle

Helen: Neil, Howie and your father just got back from the football game at the high school. Please tell everyone it's time to eat.

Neil: Do you think we could all eat at the same time for a change, you know everyone at the table together instead of people wandering in and out?

Helen: What a nice idea. Go get everyone and I'll tell them.

(Neil exits, then returns with the rest of the family).

Helen: Neil suggested we all sit together and eat at the same time, which I think is a great idea. Thank you, honey.

Howie: He actually said something? This will be a different Thanksgiving.

Jules: There's no need to be a smart aleck. Just because he's quiet doesn't mean he's not as smart as you. You know that saying—still waters run deep. Way to go, Ace. Any other ideas?

Neil: Well, I was thinking that maybe we could go around the table and everyone could say what they're thankful for this year, and maybe also what they hope for next year.

Olga: Another great idea. I always said he was a thoughtful boy. Neil, why don't you start, then the rest of the kids, then the adults. What are you thankful for?

Neil: Well, I'm thankful that we're all together. But I wish that everyone could try and be a little nicer to each other. And maybe pay a little more attention to me once in a while.

Helen: Do you think I don't notice you? Of course I do. But you never seem like you need attention, you're always so quiet and well behaved, always getting your schoolwork done or reading or poring over your encyclopedia. And I always have so much to do, so much to worry about. But I don't worry about you. You're not demanding and needy like your brother.

Howie: Hey!

Helen: But thank you for telling me how you feel.

Howie: I'll go next. I'm thankful that I'm the smartest kid in my class. And I hope to attend Harvard, Princeton, or Yale.

Neil: But that's not next year. You didn't listen to what I said.

Howie: Who said you could make the rules? That's what I'm hoping for, so that's my answer.

Olga: That's enough, Howie. Let's follow Neil's plan. How about you, Sandi?

Sandi: This is hard. I guess I'm thankful that Eddie and I got to stay here after our mother died and after all that stuff with our father. For next year, I just wish that Grandma Olga wouldn't be so hard on me.

Olga: I don't know what you mean.

Sandi: You just seem to expect so much from me, like you want me to be perfect all the time. Sometimes it makes me feel like I can't breathe.

Olga: I just want what's best for you.

Sandi: I know that. But I'm not my mother and I can't replace her. Can't I just be myself?

Olga (With tears in her eyes): Of course you can, sweetheart.

Eddie: Can I go? I'm thankful for turkey, and steak and lamb chops, and coffee milk shakes, and Yodels and Ring Dings, and Superman comic books, and my toy soldier collection. And next year I hope I can get a new guitar.

Olga: You poor little boy, you can have anything you want.

Eddie (aside to Neil): I told you I could get whatever I want from her. I have her wrapped around my finger.

Annie: This is fun. Let me go. I'm thankful for Taffy; she's such a sweet girl.

Taffy: Woof!

Annie: And I'm thankful that Olga looks out for all of us. Next year, I hope I can take some time off from the office, maybe go to Israel.

Olga: Of course I look out for you. That's what sisters do for each other. And you should take some time off and get out of Matawan now and then.

Sadie: I'm thankful that the business is doing well, that my books balance, and that my shares of Philip Morris, Xerox, and Johnson & Johnson were all up this year. As for next year, I just wish that Olga and Charlie would stop fighting all the time. It's hard watching your brother and sister argue every day. It makes me uncomfortable because I love you both.

Helen: Charlie, while I think of it, I want to thank you for wearing a shirt and pants to dinner without me having to ask you. It makes it seem more like a holiday.

Charlie: I didn't know it bothered you or I would have gotten dressed years ago. I'm thankful for those four goonks at the end of the table. I love you kids. I hope you all stay healthy and happy. As for Olga and me, the fighting doesn't really mean anything.

That's how we communicate, always have. But she's my big sister and I'd do anything for her.

Olga: That's right. We fight because we're so much alike, stubborn but strong. But it's not a big deal.

Howie (aside to Neil): I guess that explains why she chases him around the kitchen with a knife.

Jules: We should have done this a long time ago. I'm thankful for my beautiful wife— I'd do anything to make her happy. And of course my boys, my sons. My wish? I'd like a bigger say in the business, to feel like an owner instead of an employee. (To Olga) Remember how you promised to make me your partner when I turned down that job in California?

Olga: It's a lot of responsibility, Jules. But if that's what you want, let's talk about how we can make that happen.

Helen: Thanks, Mom. I'm thankful that you do so much to provide for us all and to keep us all together. But I guess I'm like Neil—I'd like a little acknowledgement every now and then, some attention, and some recognition for everything I do for you and everyone else around here. Is that too much to ask?

Olga: No. I'm thankful every day that you are my daughter. (Olga goes over to Helen and kisses her on top of her head). But it seems that most of you have issues with me. You want more attention, or less fighting, or for me to be nicer or less demanding. Well, let me tell you, I haven't had it easy.

Howie (aside to Neil, Sandi, and Eddie): Here it comes, the Story of O.

Olga: Left with two small girls and a new business when my husband died, then the war. And what I went through when Charlotte was sick and dying I wouldn't wish on my worst enemy. So maybe that all made me tougher. I had to be tough. You can't run a business unless you're tough, especially if you're a woman. But I love you all. Maybe I don't say it, but I do, and everything I do, I do for this family. So I'm thankful for all of you, and I hope I can make you each realize that. Thank you, Neil, for making this a real Thanksgiving.

Eddie: God bless us, each and every one! (Aside to Neil): They eat this crap up with a spoon.

Of course, we never had a Thanksgiving like that. Instead, our typical Thanksgiving was like every other meal. It went something like this:

Back door slams open.

Howie: We're home from the game. Let's eat.

Helen: Tell everyone that lunch is ready, Howie.

Howie: LUNCH!

Helen: I didn't ask you to yell. I could have done that.

Sandi, Eddie, and Neil enter the dining room

Howie: You guys missed a great game. We slaughtered Keyport. Don't you care?

Neil: (Shrugs shoulders).

Eddie takes a plate of food and returns to the kitchen where he sits at the counter by himself, a stack of comic books in front of him.

Howie: Ma, I want to watch the NFL game. I'll take my food to the living room. (Howie leaves the room).

Jules (entering the room): Helen, I'm famished. Would you get me a plate with a little of everything. And extra gravy. (To Neil) What are you up to today, Ace?

Neil: (Shrugs shoulders)

Helen: If you ever break those shoulders we won't be able to talk to you at all.

Olga (entering the room): Where's Eddie?

Helen: He's sitting in the kitchen.

Olga: Does he have enough to eat?

Helen: He's fine, Mother.

Olga (sits at head of table and takes a large drumstick from the platter in the middle of the table, which she waves in one hand): Jules, I was just going over the November figures. You extended a lot of credit for Christmas goods. When are you going to start collecting?

Jules: They're all good for it. Can we give it a rest for one day? It's Thanksgiving.

Olga: Do I have to remind you whose money you're giving away? They better be good for it. And Sandi, do I have to remind you to sit straight like a lady?

Sandi: Sorry, Grandma.

Charlie shuffles in, wearing a faded undershirt with holes under the arms. His pants are unbuckled and his zipper is open.

Helen: Charlie, would it kill you to get dressed for a change?

Charlie ignores her. He piles food high upon a plate and shuffles back to his bedroom. Annie and Sadie enter the room.

Olga (screaming at Charlie): Helen was talking to you, you son of a bitch. Why don't you buy your own food for a change and stop leeching off of me?

Annie: Charlie, did you hear what Olga said?

Olga: Shvayg. Mind your own business. I don't need any help from you.

Annie: Well, Happy Thanksgiving everyone! (No one responds)

Sadie: I was listening to my radio this morning. Did you know that some people are blaming the Jews for President Kennedy's assassination?

Olga: I could have told you that. They blame us for everything.

Neil: I'm done. I'm going to watch the game with Howie.

Sandi: Aunt Helen, I'll help you clean up.

Chapter Two

My high school friends called it The Ponderosa. Like the Cartwright family ranch on TV's "Bonanza," everything about my childhood home was oversized: the biggest house in town, the biggest piece of property, the biggest family.

The house was situated at the front of 23 acres of woods and marshland purchased by my great-grandfather in a foreclosure sale in the 1930's. Two stone pillars with faux Chinese lanterns guarded the entrance to the front walk from the rural highway that ran past the property. Our only neighbors were the redneck tavern a few hundred yards to one side and the small nursing home across the highway. Along one side of the building a herd of deer statues grazed eternally in the grass, part of my grandmother's stone menagerie collection—dolphins, dogs, cats, and the brightly colored camel that stood just below the steps that led to our back door.

There were 22 rooms, all on one level supposedly to accommodate the paraplegic for whom it was built in the 1920's. With its steeply-pitched red-shingled roof, tall chimneys, white clapboard sides, and lime-green stucco foundation, the house looked like some sort of architecture experiment gone horribly wrong. Inside, there was a wide center hall that ran the length of the house, at least 100 feet. For reasons I never understood, the hallway was furnished with white wrought-iron patio furniture, complete with tropical leaf patterned cushions.

There were three distinct living areas. At the front end, four bedrooms and three bathrooms lined one side of the center hall, with a living room, dining room, and large eat-in kitchen on the other side. At the back of the house, two "apartments," each with two bedrooms, a living room, and a small kitchen, flanked the hall.

My maternal great-grandmother Becky and her four children (my grandmother Olga, my maiden great-aunts Sadie and Annie, and my great-

14

uncle Charlie) lived in the front end of the house. My mother Helen, father Jules, older brother Howie, and I occupied one of the rear apartments, and my mother's sister Charlotte, her husband Irving, and my cousins Sandi and Eddie lived in the other one. Most evenings, everyone ate dinner in the large kitchen, with my mother doing almost all of the cooking. And with the exception of my Uncle Irving, all of the adults worked at Sloan Products, located just behind the house. Almost all family conversation related to the business, and it was the subject of round-the-clock arguments, screaming matches, and feuds.

All the years I lived in that house, I never had a babysitter. I was never alone. Yet, it was an easy place in which to get lost. I made staying clear of the maelstrom of adult activity and conflict my life's work, and I excelled at it, to the point that I often went unnoticed. That the room my brother and I shared was at the extreme rear of the house, and as far from Olga's room as possible, made it an easy place to disappear.

Although there were many rooms, there was nothing grand or elegant about the place. Most of the rooms were modest in size, and all were packed with furniture which, too, was oversized. There were statues and figurines throughout—ceramic dogs used as door stops, lamps with toga-clad women bases, and large planters filled with fake flowers. Standing at one end of the center-island in the communal kitchen was an artificial fruit tree, with tiny plastic oranges hanging from its branches.

The walls were covered with a kaleidoscope of swirling paint and wallpaper patterns that bore no relation to the swirling patterns of the carpets. And then there were the murals, the view from a terrace over the Gulf of Naples in my parents' living room, the Japanese cherry trees and Mt. Fuji over our dinette set, the flowering branches on the bedroom walls. Much to our humiliation, my brother and I shared a pale blue room with a painting of dogwood branches and white flowers supporting sports pennants on the wall above our beds. I spent my high school years trying to hide it all under posters of the Beatles, Dylan, and Eric Clapton.

Every available surface was cluttered with *tchotchkes* and family photos. My friends loved this stuff—the hula dancer nutcracker that broke walnuts between her thighs, the nude wooden African tribal figurines, the ceramic flower whose petals opened to reveal a cigarette holder and especially the battery operated go-go dancer whose gyrations mixed drinks in the glass attached to her waist.

On either side of the house was a large lawn, each separated from the structure by a driveway, one gravel, one paved. A large sign that read "Sloan Products, Wholesale Distributors of Paper Products, Stationery, Toys and Novelties" heralded the entrance to the long asphalt driveway that led to a parking area and then beyond to the office entrance and the loading dock to which trucks came and went all day. A hose ran across the drive, causing a gas-station like bell to ring in our basement whenever a car or truck came in or went out. Sometimes we played jump-rope with the hose until one of the grown ups came running out screaming about all the bell ringing.

The back door was our main entrance, since it was closest to the office and parking lot. For a period of time, the yard between home and business was our grassy play area, with a playhouse, swings, and some ducks. When I was nine, my grandmother decided we needed a swimming pool and the whole yard was paved over. A large brick patio with umbrella covered tables and a fountain with a Greek goddess in the center led down to the pool that was surrounded by a six-foot-high white stone wall interspersed with green wrought iron gates. A statue of a small boy with a fishing pole looked over the pool. All that stone and concrete created a convection oven effect perfect for frying our pale Eastern European skin. Surrounding it all was a series of white concrete planters.

Each year, I could tell that summer was about to arrive when I saw my mother, wearing shorts and a kerchief on her head, kneeling in front of the planters, using a small gardening hoe to "plant" red plastic geraniums around the perimeter of the patio and pool.

The house, lawns, yard, and family business only covered about a third of the property. Behind the warehouse, the property sloped down to a reed-covered marsh, thick woods, and a bucolic stream called Gravelly Brook that helped give the town its name: Matawan, supposedly Native American meaning a "place where two streams come together."

There was no doubt who was in charge of our Ponderosa—my grandmother Olga. Even though she was only 5'2", Olga was an imposing figure. She was heavy, probably around 180 pounds, but not fat. More like a fire hydrant, squat and sturdy with broad shoulders, thick arms, and stubby hands. She walked with a purposeful stride, her head always erect, shoulders back, and broad chest forward, a soldier ready for battle. Her hobbies were arguing and hondling, the age-old Jewish tradition of bargaining.

Olga would tell us all the time how she built up the business with no help from men, how after her husband died she drove a truck with her sisters and carried the cartons into her customers' stores. She also reminded us on a daily basis, especially her brother Charlie and my father, that she was the boss, that she made the decisions at Sloan Products, that it was her money being spent on inventory and equipment. She yelled and cursed, sometimes in English, sometimes in Yiddish, at anyone she felt was disloyal, mainly her brother and sisters. But she also liked to laugh, play poker, and tell dirty jokes, especially to salesmen who were calling on her:

"Did you ever hear any Sophie Tucker jokes?"

"I don't think so, Mrs. Sloan."

"She always used to talk about her boyfriend Ernie. 'My boyfriend Ernie was bragging the other day about how when he's eighty he's going to get himself a twenty year-old girlfriend. And I said, Ernie, when I'm eighty I'm going to get me a twenty year-old boyfriend, and let me tell you something, twenty goes into eighty a lot more than eighty goes into twenty.' How's that?"

"That's a good one, Mrs. Sloan."

More than anything else, Olga liked to talk about herself, usually referring to herself in the third person as "Sloan" or "Sloanie." When she got going with one of her self-involved tales, Howie, Sandi, Eddie, and I would roll our eyes.

My friends referred to Olga as Grandma Ben Cartwright and they would hum the Bonanza theme whenever they saw her coming.

Chapter Three

My family's journey to '59 Freneau Avenue in Matawan is an immigrant tale. My great-grandfather Victor Ungarman was in the millinery business in Russia, a designer and manufacturer of ladies' hats decorated with silk flowers. Sometimes Olga told us that the family came from Minsk, other times it was a place called Pinsk, and still other times it was a region she referred to as Minsk-a-Pinsk. In 1906, Victor, his wife Becky, and their three small children Olga, Charlie, and Sadie (Annie was not yet born), started the journey from Russia to America, bringing with them Victor's hat patterns. Their first stop was Bremen, Germany, where they booked passage on a ship to New York. But Charlie came down with scarlet fever, and the family was quarantined in Bremen for several months. While they were stuck in Germany, Victor sent his patterns to his sister Rose and told her she should go ahead to New York and get the millinery business started. By the time Victor and his family finally made it to New York on a ship from Hamburg in 1907, Rose had the business up and running, but she told Victor that it was hers and he could go screw. They did not speak for almost twenty years after that.

When Victor and his family arrived in New York, their name was changed from Ungarman to Ungar. They settled on the Lower East Side, eventually moving into an apartment at 104 Second Avenue, between East Fifth and East Sixth Streets. Victor started his own millinery business, but, unlike his sister, he was not very successful. He mostly lived hand to mouth. A fourth child, Annie, was born, and the four children became streetwise New Yorkers, each eventually graduating high school in Manhattan.

Olga got engaged to a man named Hyman Sloninsky, a financier of sorts. Hyman served in the Army during World War I; by the end of 1918, he was stationed in Kansas City, awaiting his discharge. While there, he wrote letters daily to his "little, sweet, sweetheart Olgele darling," most on the letterhead of the Hotel Dixon, whose motto was "Absolutely Fireproof." They were married shortly after Hyman's return to New York. Their daughter Charlotte Sloninsky was born in 1920. A second daughter, Helen, was born in 1926. By that time, the family name had been officially changed to Sloan.

Charlie also fought in World War I, and then won a college scholarship to Cooper Union, but he left school after he almost blew up a lab in a botched chemistry experiment. He then purchased a black market passport under the name Lars Olson and worked on a tramp steamer for two years, his whereabouts unknown to his family. Sadie became a bookkeeper. Annie, pretty and vivacious, turned away several suitors, since her father Victor would not let her get married before her older sister, Sadie. Neither of them ever married.

When I was growing up, Olga told us that Victor astutely realized that he was likely to lose his business as a result of the Depression, so he cashed out and moved the family to New Jersey while the going was good. A nice story, but, as I later learned from my mother, it was all a lie. Rather, when the business was on the verge of going under, Olga and Charlie, the prodigal son returned, snuck into Victor's loft one night and set it on fire. Victor collected the insurance money and moved with Becky and their daughters Sadie and Annie to rural central New Jersey, where he rented a small house in the town of Freehold.

In the years before the Depression, Hyman Sloan did very well for himself in the mortgage business. He and Olga, and their small daughters Charlotte and Helen, lived in a big apartment in the Bronx across from the New York Botanical Gardens. Olga dressed in fur-trimmed silk and satin, and each summer the family rented a place in Long Branch, New Jersey, which was the Hamptons of that time. But like his father-in-law Victor, Hyman's business got in trouble during the Depression. Hyman was a guarantor on a number of large commercial notes which were in default and he was about to get sued and lose everything. So in 1935, he closed up shop and snuck off to Freehold with Olga and their girls and moved in with Victor and Becky, leaving his creditors holding the proverbial bag.

It was two years later, 1937, that Victor took the balance of his ill-gotten fire insurance proceeds and bought the house and 23 acres of property in nearby Matawan in a tax foreclosure sale. There had been a poultry farm on the property, and the chicken coops and outbuildings were intact. After the family moved in, Victor tried getting into the egg business under the grandiose name Public Service Poultry Farm. He drove into Brighton Beach a couple of times a week to sell eggs, but he never really made a go of it, the scope of his business failing to live up to the grandeur of its name. He also did some vegetable farming, but the property was mostly marsh, so that did not work either.

Hyman was struggling, too. He had trouble adjusting to the loss of his mortgage business. With Victor and Hyman's financial woes, the household was tense. Victor and Olga got into big arguments, and Hyman could not take it. He would go into the bathroom, lock the door, and read the paper in the tub for an hour until the fight blew over. Eventually, he got a job selling vanilla extract and spices to small restaurants. At some point he added paper plates and napkins to his sales list, and that was the start of Sloan Products, a name with a different ring than Sloninsky Products would have had. But Hyman was no paper salesman. Olga was always after him, yelling at him to be more aggressive, to work harder to make sales. A lot of days he was done calling on customers by the early afternoon, but he did not want to go home to get screamed at by Olga. So instead he picked up his daughter Helen after school and took her to the movies.

In 1938, Hyman entered a hospital in New York for treatment of a number of debilitating ailments. He again wrote Olga daily, giving her instructions about Sloan Products' customers and how much each should be charged. The letters always closed with an admonition to "please eat regularly, worry less and everything will be O.K." That fall, Hyman died, followed by Victor in 1941. Olga was left with a fledgling business, a big house and piece of property, and her two daughters. Her sisters pitched in to help her make a go of it. They spent the war years running Sloan Products with little or no male help, calling on customers and making deliveries to stores and luncheonettes along the Jersey shore in their small truck, dealing with gas rationing and blackouts as best they could. When

20

the war ended, business improved, and Olga started to expand, adding toys and beach supplies to the original line of paper products.

As Olga worked with her sisters Sadie and Annie to build up their business, their brother Charlie's life began to unravel. After his return from his seagoing adventures as Lars Olson, Charlie married a woman named Sophie with whom he lived in the Washington Heights neighborhood of Manhattan. They had a son named Freddy, about the same age as Olga's daughter Helen. Freddy was born with severe mental handicaps, (according to Olga's dubious version due to a doctor's mistakes in performing a forceps delivery). Freddy was institutionalized as a young child, never to be seen by the family again. Charlie and Sophie separated, although as far as we could tell forty years later, they never divorced. With nowhere to turn, Charlie moved into Olga's house in Matawan and became a salesman for Sloan Products.

After the end of the war, Charlotte and Helen each graduated from the New Jersey College for Women in New Brunswick. Charlotte was trained as a librarian, Helen as a dietician. When they married, they remained devoted to their mother. Charlotte wrote Olga each day of her honeymoon at Totem Lodge Country Club in Averill Park, New York, David and Herbert Katz, Managing Owners ("I can't tell you in a letter probably what you really want to hear. That will have to wait for the personal touch.") My parents were married in 1947 and spent their honeymoon at the Nevele Hotel in the Catskills.

After the weddings and honeymoons, Charlotte's and Helen's husbands joined them in Olga's house, where they took possession of the two rear apartments. My mother and aunt gave up the careers for which they had been trained and went to work in the family business. Irving worked as an army engineer at nearby Fort Monmouth. My father Jules was working in the city as a salesman for a textile company. When his firm wanted to promote him, which required a transfer to California, Olga told him that if he worked for her, she would make him her partner. Since my mother wanted to stay in Matawan, he turned down the California job and took Olga at her word. That promise was never kept. My father remained Olga's employee for the rest of his life, joining my great-uncle Charlie as a salesman for Sloan Products, wearing the burden of Olga's broken promise like a yoke around his neck.

Chapter Four

We may have resided in the large house, but Sloan Products was our life. The adults in my family worked incredibly hard, from early in the morning until late at night, and most weekends as well. The focus on the family business never stopped; every family conversation and every family event was somehow tied to Sloan Products--what orders had come in that day, the trucks' delivery routes for the following morning, which customers owed money, which items were selling and which were not, and what our competitors were doing. The phone in the large kitchen was an extension of the office phone system; business calls came in seven days a week, often until late at night.

With the office only 75 feet from the house, the omnipresent effect of Sloan Products on our lives was palpable. Each time we pulled up to our driveway, the large Sloan Products sign was there to remind us of the unique nature of our little world. Every member of the family was expected to work in what we called "the office." I started in fourth grade, reporting to the office as soon as I got home from school, getting paid 50 cents a day to sweep floors and re-stock shelves.

Upon entering Sloan Products, there was a counter on the right beyond which were three desks and some filing cabinets, and around the corner was my grandmother's office. The desks sat beneath a large mullioned window that overlooked the swimming pool, patio, and the back of the house. It was in this area that phone orders were taken, my Aunt Sadie did the bookkeeping, salesmen called on my grandmother and my mother, and customers were waited on. On the left was a wall bearing samples of the paper plates, Lily Tulip paper cups, and Union Camp paper bags that were the original mainstay of the business.

Past the front office was the showroom, its pegboard walls and display cases packed with samples of the toys, games, novelties, and beach supplies that comprised the rest of the inventory. After the showroom came the "packing table" where orders were processed and packed, the maze of warehouse buildings where the inventory was stored, and the loading dock where trucks were loaded and unloaded. Some of the buildings were refurbished parts of the poultry farm that occupied the property when my great-grandfather bought it. The rest were added in stages, usually by some fly-by-night contractor whom my Uncle Charlie hired on the cheap. Maybe that is why the roofs always leaked.

Every building or area had a name—the "packing table," the "middle building," the "toy building," the "cold cup building," the "hot cup building," the "bag building", the "loading dock," the "stationery aisle," the "drug aisle," and the "shed" or "red-roofed building." Due to the slope of the property, the buildings were situated on different levels, connected by a series of steep cement ramps. The concrete walls soared to heights of twenty feet or more; wooden pallets lined the floors, upon which were stacked columns of cardboard boxes full of the items we sold. The interior of the warehouses were a haven for spiders and mice, and the exterior overhangs of the roofs were home to pigeons and nests of bees and wasps.

There were speakers throughout the buildings for the intercom system which blared all day: "I need a bundle of 32 pound bags and a case of 16 ounce cold cups on the platform"; "Jules, pick up Spring Lake Variety on line 1"; "Helen, please come to the front office."

Our customers were the small mom-and-pop retail businesses of the Jersey Shore: coffee shops and delis, bars and taverns, farm stands, five-and-tens and variety stores, pharmacies, butcher shops and local markets, and especially the stores that lined the boardwalks and beachfront avenues—souvenir shops, surf shops, and snack bars. On any given day, Sloan Products' trucks or vans could be found up to 100 miles from their base in Matawan, anywhere from Sandy Hook at the north end of the shore to Long Beach Island in the south.

The scope of the products we sold was immense. I used to tell my friends that we sold everything except pre-fabricated houses. The paper supplies included cold drink cups, hot drink cups, paper plates, napkins, toilet tissue, paper towels, cardboard carry-out trays, paper bags, pizza boxes, Chinese take-out containers, and rolls of butcher paper and brown "craft" paper. We carried Styrofoam cups and trays, plastic forks, spoons and knives, aluminum containers and "steam table trays," and rolls of aluminum foil and plastic wrap.

Then there were the "janitorial supplies": light bulbs, drums of floor wax, ant traps and spray cans of "Raid," metal and plastic garbage cans, plastic trash liners, liquid hand soap and small bars of "motel" soap, mops and brooms, metal and plastic pails and buckets, fly swatters, mouse traps and rat traps, and even feather dusters.

Sloan Products could provide the decorations for any party or holiday—streamers and crepe paper in a wide assortment of colors, banners with slogans such as "Happy Birthday" or "Happy New Year," paper tablecloths with matching plates, cups, and napkins, party hats and noisemakers, and of course a choice of coordinating gift wrap, ribbons, and bows. There was also an extensive inventory of Christmas tree ornaments and Santas of all shapes and sizes.

An entire building, the "toy building," was devoted to the company's toy and game inventory. We carried Milton Bradley and Parker Brothers games and puzzles, Venus Paradise coloring sets, paint sets, craft sets such as weaving looms, dolls and stuffed animals, Playdoh, chess and checker sets, the complete Wham-O line (hula hoops, Frisbees, Nerf balls, and Silly Putty), Duncan yo-yo's, footballs, baseballs and softballs, playground balls, and pink "spaldeens." There were shelves piled high with novelties, the small items that lined cashier counters at five-and-ten's and variety stores: plastic rings and bracelets, squirting flowers and joy buzzers, chattering teeth and miniature Slinky's.

One of the buildings had a cellar in which the school supply inventory was stored: notebooks and binders, lined paper and pads, construction paper, envelopes, folders, book covers, lunch boxes and thermoses, pens and pencils, rulers and compasses, paper paste, rubber cement, Scotch tape and Elmer's glue.

Behind the packing table were four aisles with floor-to-ceiling shelves on each side. This area held smaller-sized items sold by the dozen, rather than the large cartons stacked high in the other buildings. Here you could find batteries and flashlights, Crayola crayons, coloring books, playing cards, and an entire aisle of "drugs," items such as toothpaste and

24

toothbrushes, aspirin, shampoo, deodorant, Alka Seltzer, and sanitary napkins and tampons.

My parents and great-aunts had an encyclopedic knowledge of the inventory—where everything was stored and how much we were charging for each item. For most of my childhood, I was assigned to work with my Aunt Annie at the packing table, helping her fill small lot orders and packing them in boxes for delivery. Although she called me "cookie" when we were in the house, and always greeted me with a smile and a hug, in the office Annie was a muttering grouch with little patience for my questions about where I could find some obscure item I needed to complete an order.

One time when I was about 12, I was filling an order that included "1 gross of XXXs." "Aunt Annie, where can I find a gross of XXXs?" Annie gave me a look of disgust and started walking through the showroom towards the front office, grumbling under her breath. I scurried to keep up as she led me to Olga's office where she opened a locked metal cabinet. "Here" she said, handing me a box containing 144 condoms.

From May through Labor Day, everything revolved around our beach supply line of products: beach chairs and umbrellas, rubber beach sandals we called Zories, plastic pails and shovels, inflatable rafts and swim tubes, Styrofoam surfboards, beach balls, ice chests and coolers, Coppertone and Sea 'N Ski suntan lotion, sunglasses, plastic wading pools, and even crab traps and fishing nets. During this time of year, the whole family turned into a bunch of amateur meteorologists, since the level of success for the whole year depended on good beach weather in the summer. Rainy summers were a disaster, and during heat waves Olga was sure to complain "When it's too hot they stay in the water, they don't go up on the boardwalk to buy."

During the height of the summer season—from the close of the school year in June to Labor Day weekend—the workload at Sloan Products was brutal. Our main competitive advantage was guaranteeing next-day delivery. Each Monday, my father would be "on the road" for 12-15 hours, calling on his beach customers to take orders to replenish their stock of whatever they had sold over the busy summer weekend. My mother and Olga would also be "on the road" for much of the day to call on Olga's key longtime customers. My mother would then race back to Matawan, where she typed up her day's orders. Around this time, my father would stop at a phone booth and call in his orders to my mother for typing, as well. After a dinner break, the adults and the company's drivers (and, when we were teenagers working at home, the four goonks, as Charlie called us) would go back to work until 10:00 or 11:00 at night to fill the orders and load the trucks so the customers could receive their deliveries the following day. It was hot, dusty work, often involving climbing ladders to retrieve heavy cases stacked near the warehouse ceiling, where the summertime temperatures were well in excess of 100 degrees. And we were all on call seven days a week to fill orders and make last minute deliveries in my father's station wagon or one of the company's small vans.

Olga was a stubborn negotiator. Periodically, a real estate developer would stop in the office to attempt to buy the fifteen acres of our property that sat behind the house and warehouse. Her response was always the same. "Do you have $15 million? Because unless you have $15 million, I have nothing to say to you."

Olga did not believe in owing money. She ran Sloan Products without a bank line of credit, and she insisted on paying the company's suppliers immediately. She expected the same from her customers, although many of Sloan Products' established beach business customers were extended credit to buy their beach supply inventory in the spring, and were not expected to pay in full until later in the summer season. Around July, Olga would start her annual browbeating of my father about the rate of collections from his summer customers, continually reminding him that she had laid out tens of thousands of dollars to her suppliers and how he needed to start bringing in cash.

As summer was winding down, the focus of the business shifted to back-to-school season and the sale of school supplies. Then on to Halloween decorations and costumes, followed by the big Christmas toy and decoration season, and a final flourish for New Year's decorations and party supplies. The only lull in the business came in early winter, but in February came Toy Fair, the large annual trade show in the Toy Building at 200 Fifth Avenue in New York City. My parents and Olga

26

would spend several days at Toy Fair, visiting toy manufacturer reps and returning to Matawan each evening with bags full of catalogues and samples of new toys. As spring approached, there was a brief flurry for Easter, and then the summer season began again with pre-season sales to the shore customers. At each of these seasonal changes, my mother spent a Saturday re-doing the showroom.

Operating Sloan Products in the pre-computer age was not easy. Everything was done manually. After my mother typed the orders, the order forms went to Annie, who filled the small lot portions. Lists of the bulkier case goods were given to the drivers, who started gathering these large items and brought them to the loading dock. Then the orders went to Sadie, who "extended" the bills by filling in the prices per item and calculating the totals based on the size of the orders. My mother then took all the completed order forms and arranged them in delivery sequence for the two or three trucks that would be in service the following day. Charlie or my mother supervised the loading of the trucks, making sure that the correct number of cartons for each customer made it onto the trucks. At night, my mother would post the total dollar amount of each of the day's deliveries into a general ledger which reflected the purchases and payments of each of the company's many customers. At the end of each month, my mother prepared and mailed statements to each customer advising them of the amounts they owed.

The payroll was also prepared manually, and was always paid in cash. Each Wednesday, Sadie calculated each employee's weekly salary, overtime, and withholding for the prior week and determined the total amount of cash needed (and the mix of denominations) for payday. My mother or Annie went to the Farmers' and Merchants' Bank in downtown Matawan and returned with a large zippered envelope full of money. The cash was then doled out into small gray pay envelopes, each of which had the employee's name and respective pay and withholding information written on the outside.

In addition to our family members, Sloan Products always had at least two other employees, truck drivers who lugged the heaviest items of the inventory on and off trucks and around the warehouse and then made deliveries in our two large trucks. In the summer season, high school or college students were hired, and sometimes an additional driver, too. The one constant was Sam, who worked for us my entire life. Sam was a tall black man, 6'4", slim, muscular, and handsome. He was strong and graceful, able to lift the heaviest cases of paper goods or bundles of bags over his head and toss them onto large stacks with incredible ease. My cousin Eddie and I tried to copy him, but usually ended up staggering backwards as we attempted to press our loads over our heads.

Sam was reliable. He never missed work. He drove the longest, most difficult routes maneuvering through traffic and diplomatically dealing with contentious customers, but always made it back to Matawan in record time. He never said no to working overtime, often spending his evenings and weekends at Sloan Products. When he was around at lunchtime, he shot baskets with me on the hoop in our driveway. Sometimes when we were waiting for a truck to pull to the loading dock so we could start to unload it, Sam and I leaned on the handles of our hand trucks and talked.

"Neil, did you catch any Olympics last night?"

"A little of the track and field."

"I love Olympics. Running for your country, what could be better than that? Did you know that I ran hurdles in high school? Pretty good, too. Maybe if I kept at it I could have made it to Olympics. That would have been something. What about you, what do you dream about?"

"Getting out of Matawan, maybe moving to the city."

"It's not so bad here. Your parents are wonderful people."

"What about my grandmother?"

"She can be tough, and she sure does have a temper. But she's fair enough to me. What would you do in the city?

"I don't know. Maybe become a writer or a teacher. Do I look like a college professor?"

"Well, you need to put on a clean shirt. But I could see that. Probably beats loading and unloading trucks. Here comes a big load. Better get back to work."

Olga rarely could remember Sam's name. She simply referred to him as "the shvartza."

Part II

Welcome to My World

Chapter Five

I was born in October, 1953. I am told that on the day of my bris in Monmouth Medical Center, when I was eight days old, I was placed in a recovery room after the circumcision was performed while my parents and the rest of the family greeted their guests in another room. Unheard, I screamed and screamed, to the point that my ritual wound started to hemorrhage. In the months that followed my birth, numerous photos were taken of me in the fat arms of Hodgie, our family's baby nurse, but there are almost no pictures of me with my parents.

According to my mother, I was an easy baby and toddler, chubby, curly-haired, and content. My cousin Sandi, three years older than me, adopted me as her living plaything, pushing me around in her doll carriages, and the attention she gave me permitted my mother to focus on the numerous demands that the other members of our large household placed upon her.

My mother, young and beautiful, her long brown hair pulled back in a ponytail, was constantly rushing between the house at 59 Freneau Avenue and the office, attending to the needs of others, whether it was cooking prodigious amounts of food for our large family, responding to Olga's numerous requests, assisting in the care of my great-grandmother, working in the office, or posting to the Sloan Products' ledger at night.

While my mother seemed ever-present, yet distracted by all her responsibilities, my father's presence in the house was peripheral. He was tall, overweight, and balding. Early in the morning, he could always be found drinking a large cup of coffee and reading The Daily News. He left for the day around the same time we left for school, loping to his car, catalogues under his arm and a cigar in his mouth, as he prepared to criss-cross the Jersey Shore calling on his customers, plying the wares of Sloan Products, a peripatetic 20th Century Jewish peddler.

All day and into the evening, cars and trucks pulled in and out of the Sloan Products' parking lot. When we played in the yard, there was always a steady stream of customers, salesmen, and truck drivers entering and exiting the nearby door to the Sloan Products' front office. Over the course of the day, Olga, her sisters, Charlotte, and my mother constantly walked back and forth on the sidewalk that connected the house and the office.

At dinner, Howie, Sandi, Eddie, and I would eat together, but the adults wandered in and out, eating when they pleased. While we ate, the business phone kept ringing and our meals were punctuated by conversations with customers who were calling to place orders: "Helen, Abe Schatzow wants to know if we have forty-eight inch canvas rafts in stock?" "Yes, we have a truck coming your way tomorrow. What do you need?" "They're $10.99 a dozen, but I can take off an extra ten percent if you take a gross." Dinnertime was also where the window into the war between Olga and Charlie first opened to us, their yelling and screaming a precursor to the escalation that would follow in the years to come.

My father usually returned at night exhausted from his long day on the road after everyone else had eaten dinner, plodding from his car and then slowly making his way up the back steps to the house, where he ate by himself while my mother served him. My father's evenings were spent sleeping in a large chair in front of the television in my parents' bedroom, while my mother worked on her Sloan Products' bookkeeping chores at our dinette table. In the middle of the night he was apt to be wide awake, reading some detective novel in bed.

My memories of all this activity during the early years of my life are punctuated by a collage of images—waddling across the large lawn after Sandi and Howie in my snowsuit, playing on my wooden red rocking horse on the screened-in porch that ran along one side of the house, chasing the ducks in our backyard, dipping my toes in the waves as they lapped on the sandy shore of Bradley Beach, sitting in the bathroom that my parents, my brother, and I shared, wrapped in a thick towel after Howie and I finished taking a bath.

I learned early on that having a long driveway and a parking lot was pretty special. When I was two or three, I got a bright red tractor/tricycle. It had a small switch on the side that, when flipped, created a loud whirring noise that increased the faster I pedaled. I pedaled my toy tractor up and down the long driveway as fast as my small legs would allow, trying to make the sound louder on each pass by the house.

The parking area was also home to the four or five cars the family owned. My father was constantly moving our cars around the lot, often taking them back to our own gas pumps located near the Sloan Products' loading dock where he would fill them. On a handful of occasions, he called to me--"Come here, Ace"--and positioned me in his lap as he pulled his new 1957 DeSoto (complete with push button gear shift) back to the pumps. He would let me think I was steering the car, although he always had a finger or two on the wheel. For me, those were the best moments.

My memories of the older relatives in the house from my earliest years are fuzzier. There was my great-grandmother Brocha "Becky" Ungar, who looked like the farmer's wife in Grant Wood's painting "American Gothic," only older and more withered. She would sit on one of the couches in the long center hallway of the house or, more often, lie on the hospital bed in her room, ringing a large brass bell and calling in Yiddish whenever she wanted or needed one of her daughters or grand-daughters.

Then there was my Aunt Charlotte, wearing shorts and a white blouse tied at her midriff, always in a hurry as she raced around the office. And her husband, Irving, an engineer for the army at nearby Fort Monmouth, taking evening walks after he got home from work, smoking a pipe and swinging his arms to match his elongated gait.

In those days, nothing seemed odd about the fact that I lived with so many relatives, or that they all worked in a business located behind our house, or that we had no neighbors. Our insular world was all I knew. But when I started attending school, I started to realize that the way we lived was different from all the other kids I met.

My cousin Eddie (born in June 1954, eight months after me) and I were sent to a Jewish nursery school in the adjacent town of Keyport when he was three and I was four.

Unlike Matawan, Keyport had a number of Jewish families, many of whom owned stores in that town's larger shopping district. They became my parents' circle of friends: Sam and Adeline Siegel, who owned Vogue Dry Cleaners; Hy and Evelyn Schwartz, who owned Feigenson's Shoes; Al and Selma Goldman, who owned Keyport Army and Navy; and the rest of the Keyport Jewish crowd, the Sahners, the Waffenfelds, the Goldsteins, the Kleinbergs, the Rudnicks, and the Popicks. Their children were our nursery school classmates, and that was when I started to notice something about each of them. The only adults in their homes were their parents, and they lived in single family houses on streets lined with other single family houses. They had neighbors and playmates on their blocks, some of whom were Jewish. Their parents' businesses or offices were located elsewhere, and business was not conducted at the dinner table. They only had a few toys, neatly placed on their bedroom shelves. They took family vacations at the shore during the summer.

Even at that early age, I spent my nursery school days a million miles away, lost in my own thoughts. While my classmates napped during rest time, I stared at the ceiling, pre-occupied. When Mrs. Goldberg roused the other children, I was still lost in space until she came over to my mat calling "Neil, Neil, rest time is over."

A good portion of my daydreaming was spent trying to comprehend the differences between me and my classmates. And I was noticeably different. Howie, Sandi (born three months apart in 1950), and Eddie were my only playmates in our own little world, the large house and property our private playground. Our long driveway was cluttered with our scooters and wagons, the yard filled with a playhouse, sandboxes, wading pools, and swings. And those ducks. The long screened-in porch was home to our rocking horses, toy trucks, and Sandi's doll carriages. Irving set up a large Lionel train set for us in the basement. We wore matching cowboy and cowgirl outfits with holsters and cap pistols, or Davy Crockett hats, or football and cheerleader outfits. In the winter, we played King of the Hill on the piles of snow left by the plows that cleared the Sloan Products' parking lot. In the summer, we would wade in Gravelly Brook at the rear of our property.

We also learned about the family business at an early age. We had free rein to run through the office, showroom, and warehouse. As soon as we were able, we were taught to sweep the floors and to hang bagged toys on the pegboards that lined the showroom. We learned how to pack a box so the contents would not shift, how to use a hand truck, and how to load a truck or station wagon so that every inch of space was utilized. We quickly understood that you answered a ringing phone by saying "Hello, Sloan Products." And we were taught the fundamental law of a wholesale business—avoid breaking a dozen at all costs because you can only sell in round lots.

There were other lessons, as well. I realized at an early age that there were family secrets, things that were discussed in Yiddish among the adults as soon as I entered the room. I learned not to interrupt during heated conversations about the business and to stay clear of Olga when she was in the midst of one of her rants. But there was one lesson I mastered from the earliest age, the thing I could do better than anyone: I learned to watch it all from a safe distance.

Chapter Six

It was not merely that there were so many of us or that almost all of the adults worked together in the family business that made life in our house especially unusual. There were the odd personalities and peculiar interactions of the four Ungar siblings.

Sadie and Annie were always a pair, my two great-aunts, the youngest of the four Ungar children. Recently, a cousin told me that he never knew who was Sadie and who was Annie, and he was terrified that he would be left alone with just one of them without any idea of which one it was.

My great-aunts lived their lives in service, first to their parents, then to their older sister Olga. But more than anything their lives revolved around Sloan Products. Other than going to the beauty parlor, the bank, or the post office, or to ferry Olga around to local errands, Sadie and Annie rarely left 59 Freneau Avenue. I cannot remember them ever going to the movies, and they only went to restaurants if the entire family was going out to eat. And I can only recall them taking vacations on a handful of occasions.

Sadie was plain, with mousy brown hair and thick legs. She was generally quiet, although she was quick-witted when she chose to speak. She had an amazing facility with numbers, able to add long columns of figures in her head at incredible speed. She spent every working day hunched over her desk in the office, preparing invoices for the day's orders, and guarding her trove of index cards on which she kept track of the cost of every item in Sloan Products' vast inventory. She read The Wall Street Journal religiously, hunched over the stock tables every morning while she drank a mug of Ovaltine. Sadie rarely spent money, choosing instead to invest almost every cent she made in Philip Morris stock, with an occasional investment in Xerox or Johnson & Johnson. During snowstorms, Sadie would go out in a nightgown, galoshes, and a fur hat with large earflaps to sweep the snow off the sidewalk connecting the house and office. On Sundays, she could be found glued to the morning news talk shows from which she could always find support for her theories about worldwide conspiracies against the Jews. She would go off like clockwork at Sunday lunch:

"They're blaming Jewish scientists for helping the Russians win the space race."

"Who says? That makes no sense," my father responded. "Are you sure that's what they said?"

"I just heard it on the TV. They couldn't say it if it wasn't true."

"Which show?" my mother asked.

"What difference does it make? It was right on the TV."

Unlike her sister Sadie, Annie never discussed politics or the stock market. She was the most attractive of the Ungar women, small with curly hair and a sweet disposition. She loved animals and little children. She called each of us "cookie," and demanded a hug whenever she saw us. Until she got in the office. As soon as she entered her workday world, she turned into a screaming harpy, pacing up and down the warehouse aisles muttering. Eddie and I often worked under her supervision, and she tormented us. Annie told us constantly that we were packing boxes the wrong way, or sealing them incorrectly. Whenever Annie was looking for an item for an order, she repeated the name of the item over and over until she found it. One year we carried a stationery item called "I'm A Pad." Whenever an order came in for the pads, Annie could be heard walking around chanting "I'm a pad, I'm a pad, I'm a pad." Eddie and I followed her around, barely able to muffle our laughter, as we mimicked her: "I'm a plate of spaghetti," "I'm a banana split."

Sadie and Annie were always caught in the middle of the Olga-Charlie war. They invariably came to Olga's defense, but she was almost always dismissive of their support. But when Olga was out of sight, Sadie and Annie checked up on Charlie to make sure that he was all right. They rarely offered opinions about anything in Olga's presence, clearly fearful of receiving her rebuke.

During my childhood, Annie was the only one of the three Ungar sisters with a driver's license. She was a tentative driver and drove sparingly, mostly to take Olga to the supermarket or hairdresser or to go to the post office or bank in downtown Matawan.

On those rare occasions when they were out in the real world, Sadie and Annie were always together, two middle-aged women walking with arms interlocked. The few times they took vacations, they traveled together as part of tour groups, to Hawaii, and a couple of Caribbean cruises. One year, they took a cruise with Charlie, the only time I remember Charlie taking a vacation. He took 16 millimeter movies of the trip, but somehow managed to load the film in such a way that the movies only played in reverse: here's Sadie and Annie walking backwards up a staircase, there they are strolling backwards around the deck of the ship. The most memorable part of the film was one scene where bathing-suit clad Annie and Sadie were playfully flirting at the water's edge with two men. It was the only time I ever got a glimpse of what their lives might have been like if they had not been serving life sentences at Sloan Products. Yet, notwithstanding all the years I lived with them, I never had the foggiest notion of what Sadie and Annie wished for, what their dreams and aspirations were, or what would make them truly happy.

Unlike his sisters Sadie and Annie, who subverted their personalities and desires in deference to their older sister Olga, my great-uncle Charlie was just weird. Short and fat with unkempt curly hair and what always seemed like a two-day growth of whiskers, he walked around the house in baggy tank tops and sagging boxer shorts. If company was coming, he had to be cajoled to put on a shirt and a pair of pants. He never wore a coat, his sole concession being a worn-out cardigan sweater that he only put on during the coldest days of winter. He constantly waddled between the large kitchen and his bedroom directly across the hall, carrying glasses of tea and plates of the salami and eggs that he cooked for himself which he ate while sitting on his bed. He rarely ate with the rest of the family, and spent every evening sitting alone in his room watching television.

On Charlie's night table stood a number of toy soldiers, purloined from the sets that Eddie and I collected. He always kept a large bag of coffee-flavored candies in the drawer, which he was constantly feeding to Taffy, the family dog. Also on the night table was the long shoehorn he used to put on his shoes, since he was incapable of bending over and reaching his feet.

When the grass needed mowing or leaves needed to be raked, Charlie drove around Matawan's black neighborhood, calling to men on the street to see if they wanted "to make a few bucks." He was always showing up with down on their luck looking men who seemed as if they were ready to keel over at any moment. At the end of the day's work, Charlie handed them a paltry few dollars, oblivious to the derisive stares he got in return.

On one of his drives around town, Charlie met a man known simply as Melzer who became Charlie's contractor of choice. Melzer was a feeble-bodied African-American man who looked like he was at least 80 years old. He had no teeth and always had a chewed up cigar stub hanging from the corner of his mouth. Melzer became a fixture around our property, performing jobs for Charlie on the cheap. Invariably, the work Melzer performed had to be re-done by someone else.

Charlie referred to himself as Unk or Unk Charlie, and he called Howie, Sandi, Eddie and me the four goonks. He told me often of his plan to have Melzer build two two-family houses, one on each of the large lawns on the sides of our house. "There's plenty of room for two houses. Why spend money to live someplace else when we have all this room? When you goonks get married and have kids, there's room for them, too. That way, you can all stay together. You've got everything you need here. Here, look." He would then proceed to take a piece of paper and draw a crude map of the property with two houses penciled in on either side of the existing house.

Charlie and my father comprised the Sloan Products' sales force. Even though the toy and beach supply portion of Sloan Products' business had become the most lucrative, Charlie refused to sell any of it. He specialized in selling paper bags, rolls of butcher paper, and metal garbage cans at ridiculously low margins to small delis and farm stands scattered through the pine barrens of central New Jersey. The remoteness of his customers, and the resulting distances that the company's trucks had to travel to make their deliveries, only compounded the problem. He drove a big Ford Country Squire station wagon that he never washed—it was dusty and smelly inside, with paper samples strewn all over. He careened around hard to find country roads like a madman. On at least three occasions, Charlie had collisions with deer that severely damaged his car.

When Charlie was in the office, he sat at his paper-strewn desk, trying to place phone calls to order merchandise without Olga hearing him. His buying patterns had more to do with getting under Olga's skin than with any particular business purpose.

Other than driving around to see customers or to hire laborers, Charlie left 59 Freneau Avenue even less frequently than Sadie and Annie. He did not join us when the family went out to eat. He did not go to town, or go shopping, or go to the movies. He did not accompany his sisters when they went into the city to see a show, or when they went to visit relatives. Other than the one cruise that he memorialized in reverse, he never took a vacation. In the house, he spent most of his time either in his room or in the kitchen which was only a few steps across the hall. I did not understand his life at all.

And then there was Olga. If we were Italian, she would have been the Don of our family, despite the fact that she was a woman. Olga demanded complete obeisance from all of us, but especially from her brother and sisters. She had a pathological fear of failure, and was tough as nails in running the family business.

Even though her husband Hyman died at a young age, Olga never spoke about him with any sentimentality or melancholy. And despite the fact that she was also young when he died, she never showed any interest in having another man in her life.

Olga had a special gift for rubbing salt in wounds, reminding members of the family of the very things that haunted them most. She repeatedly told Charlie to go back to the wife who had thrown him out, or exhorted Sadie and Annie to find husbands of their own. Olga constantly reminded my father that Sloan Products was her company, each time dredging up the memories of her broken promise to make him her partner. But perhaps the cruelest was the way that Olga always itemized her late daughter Charlotte's perfect attributes in front of my mother

38

without ever mentioning my mother's special talents and lifelong devotion.

Olga was also a master of the well-turned Yiddish curse. When she got off a good one, she beamed with pleasure. But if one of us kids asked what she had said, she would just smile and shake her head. She told her brother and sisters on a regular basis to "*gai kocken ahfen yam*," loosely translated as "get out of here," but literally meaning "go shit in the ocean."

Olga's *gai kocken ahfen yam* taunt was consistent with a trait she shared with her Ungar siblings, a pre-occupation with bowel movements. Each of them was constantly asking Howie, Sandi, Eddie, and me "Have you gone poops today?" You could be behind a locked bathroom door, and Olga would still knock, asking "Are you making poops?" It was as if the four of them believed that all matters of health stemmed from regularity. Anytime someone in the house was not feeling well, Sadie was sure to suggest a "high colonic," her term for an enema, as a surefire cure. "Neil, you're looking a little pale. How about a high colonic?" The whole atmosphere was enough to clog you up for life. To this day, a knock on the bathroom door is guaranteed to make me break out in a cold sweat.

Chapter Seven

In sharp contrast to the Ungar siblings, there was nothing especially unusual about my parents, nothing except the fact that their circumstances left them with little control over their day-to-day lives. To me, it seemed like my parents lived in a penitentiary for which Olga served as the warden.

As a young woman, my mother Helen was stunningly beautiful, tall and lithe with dark brown hair that fell onto her shoulders and dark eyebrows that framed her pale face. Although she was born in New York City, Helen Sloan was a small town girl, having moved to Freehold when she was eight and to the large house in Matawan when she was ten. She lived there for the next sixty-seven years.

Helen was smart, too, valedictorian of her small class at Matawan High School. She excelled at the New Jersey College for Women in New Brunswick, where she was trained as a dietician. After college, she commuted from Matawan to downtown Newark, where she worked on the staff responsible for running the restaurant and food service at Bamberger's flagship department store.

My father Jules was also a New Jerseyan, born and raised in New Brunswick, the second oldest of the four children of Harry and Lena Selinger. It was a modest background. Jules' grim-faced and stern father was an insurance salesman for Metropolitan Life, his clientele consisting mostly of working-class Jewish families. Lena, also humorless like her husband, never had a job outside the home. After high school, Jules worked in his uncle's haberdashery store in New Brunswick during the day and attended Rutgers at night. He still had a couple of years left in school when he was drafted to serve in World War II in the Air Force. During the war, Jules was trained as a photographer. Initially stationed in England, he was the reconnaissance photographer on bombing missions over France and Germany. Despite his training, he never picked up a camera again after the war.

Like my mother, as a young man Jules was tall, thin, and good looking, his already thinning brown hair combed back just so. When he returned to Rutgers after the end of the war, my mother was a young coed at NJCW, Rutgers' sister school. They met and fell in love. They were married in May 1948 on the lawn at Olga's house. It was a formal wedding, my father decked out in tails and a top hat, my mother in a flowing satin gown. In the wedding photos, the old chicken coops on the property are visible in the background.

I was fascinated with my parents' pre-marriage life. My mother kept boxes of old photos in the breakfront in our living room. I would spread them out on the floor and stare at them, especially the pictures from her college years. There were formal shots from college balls, with my mother's dance cards for the evening attached at the corner, and casual snapshots of my mother and her bobby-sox clad classmates laughing and having fun. At some point I learned that my mother adopted a new identity at college, telling her classmates that her name was Lee Sloan.

There were fewer pictures of my father, but in a far corner of our basement there was a light box mounted on the wall covered with the aerial photos my father took during the war, and shots of my father and his uniformed buddies leaning against their bombers. I snuck down there often to look at them, my father thin, young, and handsome, seemingly so self-assured in the middle of the war. My father never liked to talk about those pictures.

After their wedding, Helen and Jules moved into one of the apartments in the back of Olga's house "temporarily." Jules commuted to Manhattan, where he was working as a salesman for a textile company; Helen commuted to Newark, where she worked at Bamberger's. It was at this point that Jules' firm wanted to transfer him to California, and Olga offered him a partnership in Sloan Products as an inducement to stay in New Jersey. Instead, he remained Olga's employee and tenant for the next thirty-seven years, treated like he was an outsider to the family. Olga paid my father a sales commission for the orders he brought in, but he was never permitted to see the books which showed how profitable the business was; the profits were Olga's and Olga's alone. The partnership she offered to Jules to keep Helen from moving to California was never offered again.

Even though Olga did not permit my parents to share fully in the success of Sloan Products, they spared no effort. My mother woke at 5:30 every morning, made breakfast for my father, made our school lunches, and drove the four of us to school. She was in the office by 7:30 or 8:00 every morning, where she worked all day, her calming presence keeping the whole operation from falling apart as Olga and Charlie bickered. She cooked dinner for all of us every night, although she rarely ate any of it. At night, she fought to keep her eyes open as she sat at our dinette table, typing the day's orders and manually posting the day's sales into the general ledger. At the end of each month, she spent an entire weekend writing out and mailing account statements to the hundreds of customers of the business. As far as I could tell, my mother subsisted on butter crunch ice cream and the cup of instant coffee she had each night before she went to bed.

Even with all this, Helen also managed to be a scout den mother, president of the PTA, organizer of the snack concession at my brother's little league games, leader of the annual school bazaar, writer and director of the Hanukah show at our temple, driver of the four of us to our various activities, and chauffer to Olga on her endless shopping trips. Helen never said no to anyone, she never turned down a task. Mostly, though, Helen spent her time trying to prove to Olga that she was as good a daughter as her sister Charlotte. She never succeeded. I cannot recall a single occasion when Olga paid a compliment directly to my mother or thanked her for all she did.

My father slumped through life as if he carried the weight of the world on his shoulders. He practically lived in his car, driving from early in the morning until late in the evening each day to call on his customers up and down the shore. Although he never smoked in the house, when he was on the road he always had a long cigar in his mouth—his car smelled like a humidor. By the time I was a young boy, my father had lost his thin physique. He ate with gusto, but was not discerning about what he ate. His only criteria was "hot and plenty of it." He could rattle off the greasy spoon lunches he ate on the road at the coffee shops and delis he called on, telling us about the cheeseburgers and hot roast beef sandwiches his customers made especially for him. His only exercise was lumbering in and out of his customers' stores with an armful of catalogues and price sheets. He read Mickey Spillane and other detective books in bed, his taste in books clearly influenced by the state of undress of the female characters depicted on the cover.

My father rarely played with us. Occasionally, he would get home while it was still light out, and if we happened to be playing ball on the lawn, he would join us for a few minutes. He hit us pop flies of immense height, or punted footballs to us in long arcs. Despite his size and weight, he was exceedingly graceful, and we could see that he must have been a good athlete when he was younger. But he seemed to have limited energy for ball playing, and these moments were always fleeting. He was a sports fan, however—primarily the Yankees, football Giants, and Rutgers football—and he fostered that interest in my brother and me. The three of us watched many games together on the TV in our parents' bedroom, my father invariably dozing off long before the outcome had been determined.

Jules was always chasing some daydream, some scheme which would enable him to get out from under Olga's rule. He bought lottery tickets every week, played the million dollar slots in Atlantic City, bought stock in risky companies, and was always trying to land the big customer that would finally confirm his worth to Olga. None of these ever panned out, only to end up with him saying to me softly "my son, for some people, everything they touch turns to gold, but everything I touch turns to shit."

My parents had no privacy. Other than going out on Saturday nights with their friends the Siegels, Olga was always present in their lives, including traveling with them on their one vacation each year. Jules made no secret that he regretted his decision to stay in New Jersey, but he often said to me "This is what your mother wanted, so what could I do?" Yet, there were times when they were walking together on a Jersey Shore boardwalk to call on a customer, their pinkies intertwined as they subtly held hands, when all seemed right in their world.

My relationship with each of my parents was complicated by the nature of our life at Sloan Products. I was in awe of my mother—her boundless energy, her patience with Olga, the kindness she extended to Sam and her other employees, her welcoming way with guests and strangers, her intelligence, her gentle personality—yet, she always seemed inaccessible to me. If I needed her to quiz me on some material I was studying for an exam, she always accommodated me, stopping her bookkeeping or typing to ask me the requisite questions. But at those moments it was somehow communicated to me that I was interrupting her, that she had so much work to do that my request was only going to lengthen her already interminably long day. As a result, I rarely asked her for anything. It felt like the best way for me to ease her burdens was to minimize the demands I placed on her.

At the same time, I harbored tremendous resentment about the lack of attention I received compared to the other members of the household. And when Olga was ranting and raving, or when she and Charlie were going at it, I could not understand why my mother took no steps to insulate Howie, Sandi, Eddie, and me from the insanity. "Why did we have to live this way?" was a question I asked myself often.

My feelings towards my father were totally different. Sometimes I felt like I was the apple of his eye—he called me "Ace" and exhibited great affection towards me. He was a kind, warm, and generous man. But we spent little time together, and certainly not just the two of us. Much of the time, he was wrapped up in playing the part of the victim, bemoaning the injustices he received at Olga's hand. It sapped all his energy, and it was hard not to feel sorry for him, if not always respectful. I could not understand why he could not summon the strength to break the hold that Sloan Products had on him. I'm sure he was asking himself, "Why did we have to live this way?" too.

Chapter Eight

My parents and the other adults in our home were pre-occupied with Sloan Products morning, noon, and night. But my parents had another distraction, my brother Howie. He had severe eczema as a child, causing him to scratch his legs raw almost every night, coupled with the allergies and asthma with which almost everyone in my father's family (myself included) suffered. Our family physician, Dr. Piper, once commented to my mother "Maybe you should throw this one back and try again." For years, my mother took Howie from specialist to specialist in Manhattan as she tried to find relief for his ailments. Then, when he was in the second grade, it was decided that Howie was too bored at school since he was much more academically advanced than his classmates. Howie was accelerated, skipping second grade completely, but leaving him a year to a year and a half younger than his new third grade peers. This presented a host of social problems for Howie on which my mother had to focus in addition to dealing with the physical hardships of his eczema and allergies. Short, skinny, smart, and Jewish was not a formula for popularity at our small town elementary school.

Howie became a master at garnering my parents' attention. One night when I was three or four, Howie came running out of our bathroom, yelling "I don't want to, you can't make me." He raced out the back door of the house and sat on the steps, his bare arms locked around his knees. It was snowing and all he had on was his underwear. My parents stood there, staring out the back window with bewildered looks on their faces. "What happened?" I asked. My mother replied, "He doesn't want to brush his teeth."

These little dramas played out all the time—tantrums, arguments, battles of wills. Just as I did when the grown-ups in the house were carrying on, the role I adopted when my parents were butting heads with my brother was to stand in the wings and observe. But as I did, I retreated into the scenery. I did not demand attention from my parents, so I rarely got it.

Howie did pay attention. We shared a room for our entire childhood. He bossed me around, but he never tried to manipulate me. In many ways, he took me under his wing. It seemed like my father was always working or exhausted, so it was Howie, always calling me Ne, who patiently taught me the rules of baseball and how to score a game, how to throw a football and swing a golf club, how to play gin rummy, chess, and Monopoly. I emulated his homework routines, even before I was old enough to have homework. I sat in the stands during his Little League games, went to his scout dinners and music recitals, and attended his drama school plays.

Chapter Nine

It was not just the unique nature of life at '59 Freneau Avenue or my idiosyncratic relatives that distinguished me from my childhood classmates. Our family vacations were noticeably different, too. Of course, we did not take our vacations in the summer like our classmates' families. Summer was the busy season at Sloan Products, seven days a week with no time off from June through Labor Day. No, from the time I was a toddler until I was eight, vacation was always ten days in February, ten days to drive to Florida and back, five days of driving crammed in a car with my parents, Olga, and my brother to spend five days at the Colonial Inn Resort Motel in North Miami Beach. Ten days for my parents' sole vacation for the year, sharing a room with their children, and with Olga who was in the connecting room next door.

There were seven or eight of these trips, but they all blur together. We stayed in motor courts or Howard Johnson (but, for some unexplained reason, never Holiday Inn) motels in Virginia and Georgia, ate dinner at orange-roofed HoJo's, and bought pecan snacks at red-roofed Stuckey's. When Howie and I got noisy and restless in the car, my father first tried to bribe us ("I'll give a quarter to whoever can keep quiet the longest") and then scare us ("when I pull this lighter a certain way, the rear seat ejects onto the highway. I'm going to pull it if you don't shut up"). Each year my mother altered our route to try and divert us at some roadside attraction: Luray Caverns in Virginia, or the glass-bottomed boats at Silver Springs, or the water ski show at Cypress Gardens.

Once we arrived at the Colonial Inn's white-columned Southern plantation front entrance, designed to look like a mini-version of Tara and to hide the standard two-story motel units behind it, we were still on the go. We visited Parrot Jungle and the Seaquarium, toured the mansion at Vizcaya, took boat rides on the Intercoastal Waterway, and played miniature golf. We ate corned beef sandwiches and pickles at Wolfie's delicatessen. Olga and my mother went shopping on Lincoln Road. Sitting and relaxing was rarely on the agenda.

On those occasions when we did spend time at the Colonial Inn's beach and pool, we were decked out in the latest resort attire. My father wore tropical patterned bathing trunks with matching cabana jackets and white rubber sandals, a cigar in one hand and a dime-store detective novel in the other. My brother and I were always dressed in matching swim outfits, the only difference being the rubber nose clips that hung on a strap around Howie's neck whenever there was a possibility we might go swimming. My mother did her best Esther Williams imitation in her fashionable one-piece bathing suits and flower adorned bathing caps. And, of course, Olga, posing every year for a photo on a Colonial Inn balcony in her skirted bathing suit, rhinestone-trimmed sunglasses, and high-heeled sandals. With her thick body and imposing demeanor, she looked like a linebacker in drag.

Even on vacation, Sloan Products exerted its presence. My father constantly checked out the Florida beach supplies and their prices to see how they compared to our inventory. Whenever we bought a drink that came in a paper cup, he lifted it up to read the manufacturer's name and cup size written on the bottom.

One of Sloan Products' main suppliers was the Union Camp paper bag company, headquartered in Savannah, Georgia. One year, Olga and my father decided on our drive home that they should stop by the Union Camp factory and pay a visit. If there is a charming antebellum section of Savannah, we did not see it. Instead, my father maneuvered the station wagon through a dismal industrial section of Savannah. Everything seemed gray—the paper mills, their tall smokestacks, and the curling smoke that drifted up to the overcast sky. The entire area smelled like sulphur. My father pulled the car into the Union Camp parking lot, when Olga announced "I think just Jules and I should go in; Helen, you stay with the boys."

As Olga and my father walked into the factory office, my mother noticed a small park across the street. "Come on, boys, let's sit in the park while we're waiting." We grudgingly put on our coats—we left the warm weather behind in Florida—and held my mother's hands as we walked to the park. It was strewn with food wrappers and empty beer bottles, weeds sprouting from the cracks in the concrete. There was nothing for us to do there, no swings, nothing to climb on. So we sat on one of the splintered benches, my mother looking fashionable in her sunglasses and kerchief, as she spent one of the waning moments of her vacation sitting with her two young sons shivering on either side of her, staring at the paper mill across the way.

Chapter Ten

In 1958, the events that were to shape the rest of my childhood were set in motion. My Aunt Charlotte got sick. I later found out that she had lymphoma, but at the time we were not supposed to talk about it or what was wrong with her or why she had stopped working. My mother and Olga escorted Charlotte to doctors in the city on a regular basis, and eventually she was admitted to Memorial Hospital that August. On weekends, my father would drive Olga, my mother, Howie, and me to the hospital. My father sat in the cafeteria with Howie and me while Olga and my mother visited Charlotte.

In October 1958, when her children were eight and four (and I was five), Charlotte died. She was thirty-eight.

The day of the funeral, my brother and I stood in the driveway watching as the rest of the family drove off. I did not understand why we had to stay behind as Sandi and Eddie went with the adults. Nor do I remember who stayed with us at the house that day. But I do remember the pall that descended on the place as the adults gathered to sit shiva— the wooden crates that appeared for the mourners to sit on, the mirrors covered with black cloth, and Olga's wailing.

Immediately after Charlotte died, the caustic side of Olga's personality boiled over. She ranted and raved, pacing up and down the long hall of the house, casting blame at Irving for Charlotte's death as if her cancer was somehow his fault. Olga bemoaned Sandi and Eddie's pitiful motherless fate, as Charlotte became Olga's sainted perfect daughter---beautiful, brilliant, and capable of no wrong. At every opportunity, Olga let Irving know that he was never worthy of Charlotte. Olga then hired an artist to paint Charlotte's portrait from one of her wedding photos. The large oval painting of Charlotte in her wedding dress hung over the piano in Olga's living room like that of a beatific Madonna.

Rarely a day passed without Olga bemoaning her fate, how no mother should have to suffer the loss of such a perfect child, and how amazing Olga was to carry on in the face of such a tragedy. Usually these outbursts ended with Olga reciting imaginary conversations she had with some customer or salesman: "He said to me, 'Sloanie, I don't know how you do it.'"

For a while after Charlotte's death, Irving focused his attention on Sandi and Eddie, even sharing his bed with them, but he detached himself from the rest of Charlotte's family. He stopped eating meals with us, usually cooking for himself in the small kitchen in the apartment he shared with his children. I often saw him sitting alone at their kitchen table, eating mamaliga, a Roumanian yellow corn mush. He still took his evening walks, and afterwards he sat in his modest living room, smoking his pipe and listening to Broadway show tunes.

Within a year of Charlotte's death, Irving became a phantom figure in our household. He started staying out until late at night and went away most weekends, leaving his children to sleep on rollaway beds in the hall outside Olga's room. Soon, Sandi and Eddie were permanently moved from their family's "apartment" at the back of the house to the front end of the house among the older generation. Annie gave up her room to Eddie and moved in with Olga, the three of them sharing a bathroom located within Eddie's new room. Sandi and Sadie became roommates. The apartment that Irving, Charlotte, Sandi, and Eddie had lived in as a family was now Irving's part-time residence. Most of the time, the door from our long hallway to the apartment was locked. Irving came and went from a separate outside entrance and the only way we could tell if he was home was if his car was parked on the gravel drive, which was on the other side of the house from the parking lot where all the other cars were kept.

Even though he still technically resided in the same house as his children, Irving ceded parental responsibility to Olga and my parents. My mother arranged and drove Sandi and Eddie to their activities. Olga or my mother supervised homework and attended parent-teacher conferences. If Sandi or Eddie got sick, Olga and my mother arranged for their care and took them to the doctor (including paying the bills). Meanwhile, Irving started taking vacations without his children, often going to the Catskills or Florida with his father. As time went by, Irving had less and less to do with Sandi and Eddie. This peculiar arrangement went on for years. The net result was that from the time they moved to the front of our house, Sandi and Eddie were raised as if they were my brother and sister. Whatever contact or relationship I had with Irving essentially ended by the time I was six.

Charlotte's death wreaked havoc in our house. Olga's already explosive temper intensified to a volcanic scale. My mother's list of responsibilities grew to include caring for her niece and nephew and trying to keep her mother calm. Olga added my father to the list of people she did not trust, another son-in-law of whom she needed to be wary. Sadie and Annie constantly attempted to tend to Olga, only to receive her scorn in return.

I started to worry. Could my mother die, too? Most often, I felt like I was lost in the shuffle, with so much attention being focused on Sandi and Eddie, or my brother and his ailments or his adjustments at school, or Olga's mental state. There were times when I even felt pangs of jealousy, particularly regarding Eddie. He was an adorable little cherub, with reddish hair, pale skin, and chubby cheeks. If someone asked about his mother, he would point to the sky and say "She's up there," always sure to result in a response of "You poor little boy" coupled with a pat on the head or a pinch of his eminently pinchable cheeks. I watched these episodes with a hunger for that kind of attention, while at the same time realizing that trading places with Eddie, or being in a situation like his, was the last thing I wanted. The whole set of circumstances left me confused, and often upset with myself for even allowing such thoughts to cross my mind.

The year of Charlotte's death, I started Kindergarten at the Hillel Academy, a private Jewish school in Perth Amboy, twenty minutes from Matawan. My mother drove me back and forth each day. No one else from Matawan attended the school, and I had no after school play dates with any of my new classmates. I was miserable at Hillel. In the middle of the school year, I was moved to Mrs. Davidson's Kindergarten class at the Broad Street Elementary School in Matawan. No one in my family seemed to notice that I was equally unhappy in our local public school, or that the adjustment of moving from an all Jewish school to one where I was the only Jew in my grade was only making my transfer all the more daunting. I knew no one and had no friends. My stomach churned each morning when it came time to get out of my mother's car and walk into the school building. Once inside, I daydreamed in class, staring at nothing in particular, totally removed from what was going on in the classroom. One day as I was daydreaming as usual, I failed to hear Mrs. Davidson telling me to do something. She punished me by making me stand on the girls' side of our daily boys versus girls game of dodge ball. I did not say a word about it to my parents.

That winter, while I was in the midst of trying to adjust to life at the Broad Street School and the entire family was dealing with grief in the wake of Charlotte's death just a few months earlier, we made our annual trek to Florida. Sandi and Eddie now joined us. The seven of us (Olga, my parents, and the four children) were loaded into my father's station wagon with our luggage strapped on the roof. As we were driving south, Olga's suitcase flew off the top of the car and bounced along the shoulder of the highway, spilling its contents. On our way to Miami, we stopped in Silver Springs, Florida to ride the glass bottom boats. I have a photo of us on that excursion. It must have been cold in northern Florida, because in the picture we are all wearing coats. My parents, Olga, and Howie are smiling, while Sandi, Eddie, and I have wounded expressions on our faces. Shortly after we arrived in Miami, I had a severe asthma attack. My mother and I spent a large chunk of our vacation with Dr. Julien, a pediatrician in North Miami Beach. This would become a pattern for me in many of our family trips.

The following fall, I started first grade. I sat at a wooden desk in the back row of Miss Parker's classroom, still staring into space and now grinding my teeth as well, until she called my name and snapped me to attention. Miss Parker was new in our school, and the only black teacher on the staff. She was strict and humorless as she strived to prove herself to the school administrators. I rarely spoke in class, yet one day when Ruth Casey, whose desk was next to mine, was whispering to one of her friends, Miss Parker singled me out and told me to go sit on the bench outside our principal's office until I learned to behave myself. I do not know if anyone told Miss Parker about the recent death in our family and the resulting turmoil in our household, but she certainly did not express any sympathy or understanding towards me. My daily dread of going to school intensified. I hoped my parents would figure that out, but I did not know how to tell them. They just seemed inaccessible, my mother burdened with her myriad responsibilities, my father exhausted and grappling with his own disappointments. When they asked me "how was school today?" I shrugged my shoulders. I could not find a way to tell them that I was worried, that I felt lost, that I daydreamed of living in a house like the Cleaver family on TV, just my parents, Howie, and me, the four of us eating dinner together each night. It was around that time that I made my mother a Mother's Day card which read "Happy Mother's Day. I love you, hope you love me, too."

My fears and anxieties during my early school years were exacerbated by a series of surgeries and overnight hospital stays: the removal of a large cyst on my leg, a tonsillectomy, and two other minor operations. Even though my mother slept in the visitor's chair in my hospital room for each of these overnight stays, I was terrified. I associated hospitals with my aunt's death, and no one thought to reassure me or convince me otherwise. And I was unable to ask for what I needed, even on the most meaningless levels, for some reason always self-constrained to do what I thought was appropriate rather than to seek what I wanted. For example, as I was recovering in the hospital from my tonsillectomy, a nurse asked me if I wanted something to drink. I was dying for some soda or juice, but I thought that in a hospital I was supposed to ask for something that was "good" for me, so I asked for a glass of milk instead. To my surprise, the nurse said I could not have any milk and brought me a ginger ale. If only everyone could have read my mind like her. One of these surgeries took place during the spring of my year in Miss Parker's first grade class. I was distressed and dejected for most of that year.

Second Grade was not much better. I was now in Mrs. Shelton's class, still daydreaming and now suffering through the humiliation of trying to learn the Palmer penmanship method. We were told that our grip on our pencils should be loose enough that someone could easily lift the pencil from our clasp. I gripped my pencil as tightly as I could, pressing hard on our lined worksheets, making my Palmer loops and curves as dark as possible. Mrs. Shelton walked up and down the aisles between our desks, reviewing our progress. When she came to me, she usually tried to lift my pencil from my steely grip, and when I resisted, she slapped the back of my hand. We fought this battle all year, and my report card bore a neat row of "C's" in the handwriting column.

One day, I was sitting in Mrs. Shelton's class working at my desk, when she said to me, "Neil, you can leave now." I had no idea why I was being singled out or what I had done to warrant my dismissal from the class. I stared at my teacher, who then said "Go on." I walked dejectedly to the cloak room at the back of our classroom, put on my coat, and left the building where my mother, Howie, and the rest of his scout group were waiting outside. My mother had obtained Mrs. Shelton's permission for me to go on a scout field trip. The only problem was that she never told me about it.

In the winter of 1961, we once again drove to Florida for my parents' annual vacation. My father loaded the seven of us and our belongings into and onto his Pontiac station wagon. As we got ready to pull out of the driveway, Charlie pointed out that our rear bumper was about an inch off the ground. My parents got out and circled the car, until my mother said "Let's take two cars." Just like that we split up the bodies and the bags, each of my parents now obligated to drive the entire way and back without any relief from the other. At every stop, we rotated children from one car to the other until we exhausted all the possible combinations and started the process over.

When I returned from vacation to Mrs. Shelton's second grade class, I made my first real friend, a playmate for me other than Sandi, Howie, and Eddie. His name was Terry Diehl, a red-headed, freckle-faced boy who lived in a small house about a half mile from us, and in between our school and home. I started going there after school, playing with Terry in his small backyard like two average second grade boys. At the end of that school year, his family moved out of Matawan and I never saw him again.

Chapter Eleven

It was during this time, 1961, that my great-grandmother Becky died. Her presence in the house had a restraining effect on Olga and Charlie, but once she was gone their battles raged daily at a heightened level. They spent every waking moment fighting with each other about the business, or some other past slights and perceived wrongs that were never explained. Olga would call Charlie a son-of-a-bitch, he would call her a cunt, she would remind him that she took him in when his wife threw him out, then the argument would devolve into a screaming match in Yiddish until it started all over again. Often, Sadie and Annie would try to come to Olga's defense, telling Charlie to stop, at which point Olga would turn on them, telling them she didn't need them, that they should go find husbands and homes of their own.

Olga and Charlie had no compunction about playing out their daily drama in front of others. Most days, the argument took place within Sloan Products. The two of them would get going in front of Sam, or the company's other drivers, or truck drivers from other companies who were making deliveries. But salesmen making cold calls to the office seemed to bring out the worst in Olga and Charlie. The scene was almost always the same:

Salesman (leaning on the office counter): "Hello. I'd like to speak with Mrs. Sloan about our line of products. Is she in?"

Charlie: "Don't waste your breath."

Olga (emerging from her office): "Don't listen to a word that son-of-a-bitch tells you. If it wasn't for me, he'd still be living out on the street where his wife threw him."

Charlie: "What did that cunt say about me? You can't believe a word she says. When we were kids, she used to stick her hand down my pants and try and play with my dick."

Olga (screaming): "You fucking liar! Why don't you get off your ass and do something around here. Go see some of your deadbeat customers. Better still, go back to your wife and your idiot son, you bastard."

Salesman (Backing out the door): "I've left some catalogues and a price sheet. Look them over when you have a chance. Have a nice day."

The dinnertime fights were the worst. Howie, Sandi, Eddie, and I would be at our usual places at the large table in the communal kitchen. Charlie, short and fat, shoeless and wearing a sagging t-shirt and boxers or a baggy old pair of pants, would shuffle into the kitchen to get some food, and Olga would start in on him, telling him to buy his own food and to stop sponging off her. The four of us sat frozen at the table, immersed in our comic books and magazines, as they screamed back and forth. Sometimes Olga threw cans of Del Monte corn or peas at him as he scurried back across the hall to his room.

One dinnertime fight was particularly memorable. Olga had just learned that Charlie had ordered a large amount of merchandise without her knowledge or permission, when Charlie happened to waddle into the kitchen.

"Who do you think you are, spending my money without asking? It's nothing but spite work."

"I'll sell every last piece that I ordered. If you listened to me once in a while, we wouldn't have so much shit in inventory. You don't know what the hell you're doing. You're lucky I came here or you would have been out of business years ago."

"You lying bastard! I saved you when that piece of shit wife threw you out. What did I do that I have to suffer so, losing my beautiful daughter and then stuck with a good-for-nothing brother?"

"That's right, Olga. The whole world revolves around you."

"Get out of here, you fucking liar. I'll kill you!"

Olga then grabbed a large kitchen knife, wielding it over her head as she started to chase Charlie around the kitchen. Charlie scampered out of the room just as Olga slipped and fell onto the table where the four of us were sitting with our mouths agape. Her weight upended the table and as she sat on the floor amidst the paper plates and food while her sisters attempted to help her up, she screamed: "Go back to your wife, you son-of-a-bitch!"

A few days later, Charlie started cutting Olga's face out of the family photos displayed throughout the house. As for me, retreating to my room where I could read and daydream of a more normal existence seemed like a good idea. Soon there was always a book on my night table, and propping myself up on my bed with my latest written escape balanced on my knees became my daily position of choice. The corner of my room where I slept was as far as I could get from the storm that raged at the other end of the house. It became my private lair.

•

Chapter Twelve

By 1962, something changed at home. Maybe it was because the gloom that hung over the house since my Aunt Charlotte died in 1958 had ever so slightly started to lift. Maybe it had to do with my great-grandmother Becky's death in 1961 after years of confinement to a hospital bed, her activity limited to ringing the large bell that sat on her night-table whenever she wanted attention from one of her daughters. But mostly it had to do with Sloan Products. After twenty-five years of struggle, the cash was really flowing, and Olga was feeling flush.

No longer content with an Oldsmobile or Buick, Olga bought a sharp-finned Cadillac Sedan de Ville for my mother to drive. Olga, Sadie, Annie, and my mother got new mink coats. And new hair color—no longer brunettes, I guess the four of them wanted to see if it was true that blondes have more fun. I was shocked when four females with blond hair walked into the back door of the house. My mother now looked like a platinum haired glamour queen, posing in her feather-trimmed yellow suit and cape in front of her navy blue and white vinyl topped Caddy or poolside in a gold lame swimsuit. We got a dog, too, a Toy Poodle named Taffy.

The house and yard also got a makeover. The room that Howie and I shared was enlarged, as was the room that Sandi and Sadie shared. My brother and I also got a new bathroom of our own, with yellow tiles, yellow sink, yellow toilet, and an etched glass shower door covered with images of swans and lily pads. The screened porch that ran the length of one side of the house, and which had been our playroom, was enclosed to accommodate the expansion of the rooms that adjoined it. Every room in the house got an air-conditioner. An old Italian painter named Joe took up residence at the house, painstakingly creating murals in many of the rooms and covering the wainscoting with a swirling, marbled effect. The walls that were not painted were covered in patterned wallpaper. The kitchen in my parents' apartment was re-modeled with new brown-faced appliances, yellow formica counters, and yellow and orange tile circles on the walls. The large kitchen was re-done, as well, with the same brown appliances, light blue formica counters, and light and dark blue tile circles on the walls. The kitchen also now had a large center island. That is when the plastic orange tree appeared.

The house renovations and painting were followed by a furniture-buying spree. Olga and my mother became regulars at furniture showrooms on New York City's lower east side, but there was no unifying design theme to their purchases. My new room was crammed with contemporary light brown wood furniture more suited to a married couple than two boys, including a "Hollywood" bed that consisted of two twin mattresses affixed to the same headboard with no space between them. I spent the next five years, until Howie left for college, with his hand in my face each night. The large dining room, Olga's room, and the room Sadie and Sandi shared got new, traditional French-styled furniture, decorated with lots of fake gold leaf. My parents and Olga each got new Danish modern entertainment centers for their living rooms, with built-in stereo systems and televisions, and fold-down bars. Olga's living room also got a new curved sofa. White wrought-iron patio furniture was added to the center hallway, its linoleum floor replaced with a swirling patterned carpet. There were kitschy, modern lamps added throughout the house, but also statues and lamps featuring toga-clad maidens.

It was also during this period that our grassy backyard disappeared beneath bricks and concrete. The old barn and chicken coops were razed as Olga set out to make the whole place "classy." She realized her vision with a Roman-style swimming pool, large patio, white stone fence and planters, and more statuary including a large fountain, dolphins, a small boy with fishing pole, and a multi-colored camel. The pool became an adjunct to the Sloan Products' showroom, always filled with a wide array of inflatable rafts and pool toys that customers could view in use rather than hanging on a pegboard display wall. Statues of grazing deer appeared along the side of the house, and the stone pillars at the head of the front walk were adorned with large, bronze Chinese style lanterns.

In the midst of all this construction and decorating, I misbehaved for perhaps the only period of my childhood. Maybe it had to do with all the changes. When the excavation was complete for the foundation for the enlarged room that Howie and I were going to share, I decided that the hole in the ground would make an ideal place to play. I convinced Eddie to join me.

"Let's pretend that this is a trench during World War I. We need to hold off the Germans."

"What will we use for weapons?" Eddie asked.

"I know—grenades. Let's get some pears."

We proceeded to gather fruit from the pear trees that lined our long driveway, and then climbed into our "trench" with our pile of ammunition. We tossed grenades until we got bored and climbed out, leaving the pears and our uneven footprints behind. The following morning, the contractor arrived with a cement mixer to pour the foundation, only to find that his excavated site was full of pears and no longer level. My mother stormed into my room.

"Do you know anything about the pears and footprints in the new foundation?"

"Eddie and I were playing in there."

"You get down there right now and help clean it up." I trudged outside with my head down, where I helped the contractor remove the pears while he cursed under his breath.

I did not learn my lesson. Shortly before the backyard was scheduled to be torn apart for the new swimming pool, Howie and I decided that a small snow drift in the yard was a perfect place to practice golf shots. I took a full swing and sent a golf ball whistling through the office window, missing Sadie's head by a few inches. She rushed out of the office screaming.

"Who hit that ball? You could have killed me." She took one look at me with the golf club in my hand. "You're paying for that window, mister."

It was also around this time that the Sloan Products' check writing machine captured my attention. It looked like an adding machine, with a red-handled lever on one side. One day after school, I started playing with it like it was a slot machine, pulling the lever time after time until it jammed and would not budge. Just then, Sadie walked in with a stack of blank checks in her hand and saw what I had done to her prized possession.

"Now you've done it. You're really paying for this. It cost me $35. And you still owe us for the window."

That evening, my mother came into my room. "You have to pay Aunt Sadie for the machine you broke. Do you have any money?"

"Only what's in my piggy-bank" I had a large metal bank in the shape of a bust of Abraham Lincoln which I stuffed pennies into at every opportunity.

"Well, you're going to have to empty it. I'll take you to the bank tomorrow and they'll convert your change into bills."

The following morning I poured the contents of Mr. Lincoln's head into a brown paper bag. My mother drove me to the Farmers' and Merchants' Bank in Matawan's small downtown. When the teller asked "Can I help you" I walked to her window and triumphantly proceeded to pour all the pennies in my bag onto her counter, my pride in my savings momentarily overriding my dejection in having to part with it. A tidal wave of pennies crashed in front of the teller, their cascading noise drawing the attention of everyone in the bank. "I need to change these into dollar bills." The teller turned crimson and stared at me for a moment, debating whether she could get away with screaming at a young boy. "Put your pennies back in the bag, please. Here are papers that you can use to make penny rolls, fifty to a roll. When you've done that, come back and I'll help you." It was a lousy job, since I had thousands of pennies, and it took me days to complete. I exchanged my rolls for eighteen dollars, the extent of my savings. I handed the bills to Sadie, who took them without a word. I got back on the straight and narrow.

Chapter Thirteen

During this period, winter weekend trips to The Concord Hotel in the Catskills were added to the list of our large family sojourns (always winter weekends, as summer weekends were saved for servicing Sloan Products' Jersey Shore customers). There were three or four of these trips, the seven of us (my parents, Olga, and the four goonks) making the two and a half hour drive from Matawan in my father's station wagon. There was ice skating and tobogganing, swimming in the indoor pool, games of Simon Says led by the hotel's social director, and gorging ourselves on the never-ending supply of food. My parents posed for caricature drawings by the hotel's resident artist. We went to shows in the cavernous nightclub, seeing Borscht Belt comics like Buddy Hackett and Milton Berle. Olga took up residence in one of the overstuffed sofas in the ornate lobby, where she held court, talking about herself to anyone who would listen. It was mostly great fun, but Olga's presence and my mother's inability to escape from Olga' relentless demands for even a weekend hung like a low-lying cloud over our amusement.

My favorite memento of these trips is a photograph of me standing stiffly in my bathing suit next to Buster Crabbe, the former star of the TV shows "Foreign Legion" and "Tarzan." Crabbe was clearly on the down slope of his career, working at the Concord greeting guests at the pool. In the picture of the two of us, he looks bored and distracted. It is hard to say which of us looks more uncomfortable.

The conspicuous spending of these years was never more apparent than at our bar and bat mitzvahs. Howie and Sandi reached their milestone in a joint service and celebration in December, 1963, followed by me in October, 1966, and Eddie in June, 1967. All three events were essentially the same: a Friday night service and *kiddush* at our temple in Perth Amboy, followed by a Saturday morning service and elaborate *kiddush*, and a Sunday afternoon reception at the Chanticler, an ornate catering facility in a restored mansion in Millburn, New Jersey. Olga, my mother, Sadie, Annie, and Sandi got new outfits for each of the nine functions at Chez Mode, Olga's favorite boutique. My father and the three boys had new jackets or suits for each, as well. Even Charlie wore a suit and tie.

Although Howie, Sandi, Eddie and I were the purported stars of these events, ultimately they were about Olga and Sloan Products, an opportunity for her to showcase her success. In addition to the throng of friends and relatives that attended, there were always several tables full of Sloan Products' largest customers and the company's key manufacturer's representatives, including the regional salesman for Union Camp bags and Lily Tulip cups. Unlike our Hebrew school classmates, whose bar and bat mitzvah haul was comprised solely of checks, savings bonds and silver pens, our gifts also included shares of stock in the companies that were the main suppliers to Sloan Products.

Just because Olga started to spend more freely did not mean the family was no longer crazed when it came to money. Olga had limited faith in any one bank, so she opened accounts at dozens of banks across the county. Each month my mother drove Olga from bank to bank so she could get her interest posted on her passbooks. Charlie kept his money in the basement. One day Eddie and I were down there playing when we discovered a large paper bag shoved under some furniture. As we opened it and saw it was full of cash, Charlie came screaming down the stairs: "That's mine. Leave it alone." Sadie and Annie had stacks of unopened Sloan Products' pay envelopes locked in a closet.

The extravagance of life at our house extended to the way we ate. We were surrounded by food. It was the family obsession. The house had three refrigerators, each overflowing. Olga and Annie went to the supermarket each week and came back with 30 or 40 bags of groceries. Once every few weeks, a kosher butcher delivered an entire side of beef, cut into roasts, steaks, ground beef, and ribs. There were closets filled with canned fruits and vegetables. Every counter in the communal kitchen was covered with breads, cakes, rolls, and usually a bunch of rotting bananas. My mother cooked for the entire household every night—roast beef or pot roast or stuffed cabbage or veal cutlets or goulash or roast chicken—and if you didn't like what she had made, she would make something else. This was always accompanied by canned corn, canned peas, canned Franco-American spaghetti, canned fruit cocktail and frozen French fries.

The four children always ate together. We were allowed to read at the table, and we always had an assortment of comic books, magazines, and books in front of us as we ate. The adults wandered in and out, dinnertime spreading across the evening hours. Olga, Charlie, Sadie, and Annie drank glasses of hot tea while holding sugar cubes between their teeth. They slurped borscht and cabbage soup and then sucked on the bones my mother used to make the stock. Olga attacked left over chicken and turkey carcasses with ravenous relish, picking up an entire skeleton and gnawing at it with gusto, bits and pieces falling onto the rhinestone trimmed glasses she always wore on a chain around her neck. When she was done, she put her glasses back on, food particles sticking out from the edges of the frames.

Every meal started with grapefruits cut in half; if they were not eaten, they went back into the fridge and kept returning to the table evening after evening, as they turned puckered and brown. There was also the same salad every night. Literally. The same salad. A big plastic bowl filled with iceberg lettuce, tomatoes, and red onions, topped with a bottle of eerily orange colored Kraft Catalina dressing. Whatever was left went back into the fridge in the same bowl, only to return the next night to be "freshened up" by my grandmother who added another layer of lettuce, tomatoes, onions, and dressing on top of the wilted and congealed scraps in the bottom of the bowl. I called it the never-ending salad bowl.

My father usually ate dinner by himself. He arrived home from his long day of calling on customers well after the rest of us had eaten. He sat at the end of the table waiting for my mother to serve him. I never saw him touch the oven or the stove, or serve himself, or clear his plate when he was done eating. But late at night he could be found standing in front of the refrigerator in our apartment, cutting slabs of salami or preparing crackers lathered with butter for a bedtime snack.

We ate dinner in the large kitchen at the big table pushed close beneath the windows. Seats on the window side were prized, since it meant you could not get in or out once everyone was seated, thus relieving you of carrying things back and forth to the table. The kitchen had a center island with the stove-top in the middle, and the artificial orange tree at the end closest to the table. One side of the island had a low counter with four brightly colored molded plastic stools. For many years, Eddie sat at the counter and ate dinner separate from the rest of us sitting at the table.

We almost always ate our meals on Chinet paper plates, drank from Lily-Tulip paper cups, and wiped our mouths on Marcal paper napkins, all supplied by Sloan Products. We produced mountains of trash.

Once every week or two, we ate Chinese take-out food for dinner, or as Olga called it, "Chinks." There was only one Chinese restaurant in the area, The House of Eng, which happened to be a Sloan Products customer. Our take-out orders were immense, placed in several boxes overflowing with Sloan Products supplied cardboard pails filled with shrimp with lobster sauce, egg foo young, chicken chow mein, pressed duck, and fried rice, as well as insulated bags containing mounds of pork spare ribs and shrimp egg rolls. No one questioned the inconsistency of eating all this *treif* in our so-called kosher kitchen.

Sloan Products closed for lunch each day from 12:00 to 1:00. The adults would all return to the house to eat meals consisting of things like sour cream and berries, or herring, or cold borscht, or cottage cheese, or something they referred to as pot cheese. Every few days, my mother would drive the 20 minutes to Perth Amboy, site of the closest Jewish deli, to buy corned beef (extra fatty), roast beef, turkey, salami, bologna, sour pickles, and rye bread for our school lunches.

The house was also stocked with junk food of every kind. My mother kept a drawer in our kitchen filled with Twinkies, Yodels, Ring Dings, Hostess cupcakes, and an assortment of Drake's cakes. We had Wise potato chips and Fritos, Eskimo pies and Popsicles. There were bottles galore of Pepsi and Hires root beer, and large cans of Hawaiian Punch. And always large pitchers full of the sweetened iced tea which Olga could be found making at 3:00 in the morning.

We went out to restaurants to eat dinner en masse, everyone but Charlie. After studying the menu, Olga or Sadie or Annie would turn to my mother and ask "What should I eat?" at which point my mother would remind them what they liked. This exercise was repeated whenever we went out, the process taking an agonizingly long time, only to end when the three of them each ordered the same fried seafood platter they always had. My father invariably ordered last, and as he calculated the size of the tab we were running, he ordered the cheapest thing on the menu. Every leftover scrap was brought home. And no matter the state of Olga's war with her brother, whenever we went to a restaurant for dinner, Olga always made sure to get a meal to go to bring home for Charlie.

If one of us mentioned that there was a particular food we liked, we got inundated with it. Eddie once noted that he liked French toast. Olga started making platters of it every Sunday morning, long after Eddie lost interest. When Howie mentioned that he liked coconut cream pies, the kitchen started to look like a pie shop. I once made the mistake of saying "this is pretty good" as I bit into a prune Danish. Dozens of them were bought every week after that for years. As the cliché goes, at 59 Freneau Avenue, food was love.

Late at night, when Eddie and I were watching Creature Feature or Thriller Theater or the Twilight Zone, Olga often came in carrying a platter of broiled lamb chops. "Are you boys hungry?"

Chapter Fourteen

The loosening of Olga's purse strings was not limited to renovations, groceries, weekends at The Concord, and large catered affairs. The annual road trips to Miami stopped. In February 1962, instead of piling into my father's Buick Estate Wagon for our annual pilgrimage to Florida, we went on a cruise, seventeen fun-filled days on the S.S. Brasil from New York to the Caribbean and back. Seventeen days with my parents, Howie, Sandi, and Eddie, and of course Grandma Olga, always Grandma Olga. I was eight years old and in the third grade.

The preparation for this cruise vacation was like a troop movement. My mother had to pack for everyone, cocktail dresses and dinner jackets, bathing suits and matching cover-ups, and cruise wear, whatever that meant. We were going to miss days and days of school, so my mother saw all of our teachers to get assignments for us to do while we were away. We had our books and our Kodak Brownie cameras and my mother's 16 millimeter movie camera and a vast Sloan Products' assortment of suntan lotion. My father had his cigars and a fat billfold of cash.

I spent the weeks leading up to the cruise in nervous anticipation, lying awake in the room I shared with Howie as I tried to imagine what our trip would be like, envisioning the foreign terrain and hoping that a new locale would somehow alter our daily family dynamic, especially the way that my Olga rode roughshod over the feelings of my parents and everyone else in our extended household. As my mind raced, I tapped my fingers on the long headboard to which our adjoining beds were connected, until my brother finally yelled "Would you cut it out?"

The day of our grand voyage finally arrived. My parents decided we should take the bus into the city, so Annie and Charlie used two cars to take the seven of us and our twelve suitcases to the local bus station. The bus driver opened the luggage hatch on the side of the bus, and I threw my suitcase in as far as I could. Realizing that he would have to crawl inside to retrieve it, the driver gave me a dirty look.

My father slipped the driver some cash and he dropped us off right at the pier rather than the Port Authority bus terminal. Standing on the pier with our pile of luggage, the seven of us were like a new chapter of our family's American immigrant dream that began on the ship from Hamburg fifty-five years earlier: we had made it, we had succeeded, we had lots of stuff, and we could now afford to get back on a boat of our own choosing.

We checked our twelve suitcases and headed up the gangway onto the ship where we entered a grand room that looked like a hotel lobby. My father stepped up to the front desk and got us registered, and we were then led to a bank of elevators which would take us to our adjoining rooms. As the door to one of the elevators opened, I stepped into the chrome and mirrored compartment followed by my family. My father pressed a button and the elevator started to climb.

The elevator stopped, but I was not paying attention and did not notice what floor it was. The door opened and the six other members of my family stepped out, but as I stepped forward the door closed and the elevator started going up again. Alone in the elevator, I frantically started pushing buttons and when the door opened I got out and started walking up and down the long corridors past door after door of numbered staterooms which had no meaning to me, weaving my way through the throngs of other passengers. I started to cry.

I had no idea how long I had been wandering the halls. Ten minutes, twenty, thirty? Finally a man in a white uniform carrying a clipboard bent down to talk to me.

"What's the matter, son?"

I could barely speak. "I'm, I'm lost."

"What's your last name?"

"Selinger," I blubbered.

He flipped through the pages on his clipboard. "Selinger, here it is. Come on, I'll take you to your room."

Within a matter of minutes, still red-faced and teary-eyed, I was delivered to the room where my parents and my brother were unpacking. I ran to my mother and hugged her around the waist. "What's the matter?" she said.

I barely managed to tell my tale. I did not understand why the three of them were smiling.

"We didn't notice you were gone. I guess we just assumed you were next door with your cousins in Grandma's room." My mother then stepped next door. "Did you know that Neil was lost and wandering around the ship looking for us?"

"Wasn't he with you?" Olga replied with a grin on her face.

I did not set foot on an elevator the rest of that trip, choosing instead to race up and down the stairs while my family rode, and I made sure to keep contact with another member of my family at all times.

Our first night at sea, my father and I ate dinner together while the rest of the group fed the fishes, as they say, but soon everyone got their sea legs. Olga and my parents took full advantage of the never-ending food offerings—three meals a day, plus an afternoon tea and a late-night buffet. My father and the three boys wore white dinner jackets to the dining room, while the women wore glittery dresses. Olga and my mother even brought their mink stoles on our tropical vacation.

The four of us had the run of the ship. We raced around the deck, played bingo with the older passengers, went to movies and cabaret shows, and drank gallons of soda, milk shakes, and Shirley Temples. We performed in the passengers' talent show, a quartet singing "Winter Wonderland." At the costume ball, Howie and Sandi were dressed as salt and pepper shakers, while Eddie and I were pirates with eye-patches and fake moustaches and goatees. The night of the Captain's cocktail party, I hid behind my mother's hip as we moved through the receiving line.

Each time the ship pulled into a port, we were met by rowboats full of young boys who dove into the water to retrieve the coins that passengers threw from the deck. At each place that we visited on the trip, the seven of us took some elaborate tour, bouncing in vans along rutted roads through the rainforest in Puerto Rico, up and down the mountains of Martinique, to the old walled city of Cartagena, and to the beaches of Barbados and Nassau. It was my first exposure to poverty, as we drove past tin shacks and ramshackle villages on each of our excursions, barefoot boys and girls chasing our van with their hands out, a stark contrast to our opulent experience on board the Brasil.

As usual, my mother spent a large part of her vacation tending to Olga, helping her get dressed, escorting her around the ship, and counseling her on what to order to eat. When we arrived in a port, my mother took Olga to the shopping district where she hondled and bought like a woman possessed, amassing a huge haul of embroidered linens, china, vases, and jewelry. In Curacao, she bought my mother a ring with an aquamarine stone the size of a domino.

By the time we reached Panama, I had developed my usual vacation illness, this time a severe ear infection. I spent our train ride to the Panama Canal throwing up out the window.

My misadventure on the Brasil traumatized me. It confirmed all my worst fears about my place in the family, that I was an afterthought. Whenever I brought the episode up, everyone would have a good laugh at my expense. At some point, my mother just started saying "We're not going to have to listen to that cruise ship story again, are we?"

Missing two weeks of school to go on a luxury cruise further differentiated me from my small town, third grade classmates. To compound my discomfort, my mother convinced my teacher, Miss Mahon, that it was a good idea for her to come to my class to show our family movies of the trip. I sat in the darkened classroom with my arms folded, red with embarrassment as my classmates watched Howie, Sandi, Eddie, and me in our matching clam-digger outfits. Everyone started laughing at the scene where the ship's nurse, who had taken care of me when my ear got infected, pulled my head to her chest and hugged me. I wanted to curl up into a ball and hide under my desk. These were the same classmates who groaned every time I raised my hand to answer one of Miss Mahon's questions or picked me last for our group games during recess. The last thing they needed was more ammunition for their taunts. I felt like I was never going to fit in, and my mother was only making things worse.

One of my third grade classmates was a boy named Bobby Warren. Like many of my classmates, he was tired of hearing about our grand vacation. He came up to me on the playground one day and said "You know you're not the only one who gets to go on vacation with his family. We're driving to Florida for Easter vacation."

The first day of school after Easter break, Miss Mahon entered our classroom with tears in her eyes. "Boys and girls, I have some terrible news. The Warrens were in a horrible car crash on their way back from Florida. Bobby was lying across the back seat sleeping when it happened. He's dead."

Chapter Fifteen

If Bobby's death had an effect on my third grade classmates, they hardly showed it, or maybe I was too pre-occupied to notice. But his fatal accident and my cruise ship trauma had a compound effect on me. While I longed for a different type of life than the one I had at 59 Freneau Avenue, I worried even more. If no one noticed me when I was home, would they forget me altogether if I spent time away from the house? And when you ventured out in the world, bad things could happen, like they did to the Warrens. The net effect was that for the following two years, I rejected every opportunity to participate in activities beyond our property.

As fourth grade began, I started to develop imaginary stomach aches during the school day. I became a regular visitor to the school nurse's office, where I did my best to convince her that I should be sent home. I missed days and days of school that year. My parents signed me up for Cub Scouts, like they had for my brother. I dropped out. I tried out for Little League like Howie had, but I soon quit. I refused to return after one week of day camp. I stopped taking piano lessons after only a few weeks. When I attempted to sleep over at another boy's house, I invariably called my parents and demanded that they come pick me up. Instead, I descended further into our insular world. It was a perfect place in which to disappear.

Our house and family business were located on the outskirts of Matawan, a small town of about 2,500 people. We did not live in a neighborhood, and there were no neighborhood kids with whom to play. Howie, Sandi, and Eddie became my only playmates in our own little world. And even though we were surrounded by adults, we had the freedom to do as we wished, without supervision, as long as we stayed on our property.

We climbed the large maple tree on the side lawn and pretended it was a rocket ship. Howie, Eddie, and I played wiffle ball, football, kickball, and golf on the lawn while Sandi practiced cheerleading routines. We all played spud in the driveway. Howie and I played basketball in the room we shared, tossing our rolled up socks into the metal waste basket. The four of us used the loading dock of the warehouse as a stage, putting on imaginary shows. We lay on the floor of the long center hall of the house and had Taffy jump over us like we were hurdles on a track. We danced in Sandi's room as she played 45's on her record player that looked like a jukebox. We swam in the pool day and night. We had stacks of games direct from the Sloan Products' inventory—we played Clue and Monopoly, Careers and Risk, and Stratego and Scrabble. We painted by numbers and colored our Venus Paradise landscapes. There were yo-yo's and Slinky's, Silly Putty and Hula Hoops, Frisbees and Nerf balls. We watched TV together, "Abbott and Costello" and "The Three Stooges", the "Mickey Mouse Club" and "Wonderama", "Leave It To Beaver" and "Ozzie and Harriet." But our favorite was Million Dollar Movie, which showed the same film ten times in one week. We memorized movies-- "Yankee Doodle Dandy" and "King Kong," "Mighty Joe Young" and "Forbidden Planet," "Godzilla" and "Rodan," "A Christmas Carol," and "The Thief of Baghdad" and "The Flame and the Arrow."

And, of course, we worked together in the office, where we pushed hand trucks piled high with cases of paper cups and plates and toilet paper up and down the ramps of the warehouse at breakneck speed. Eddie and I constantly tried to outdo each other as we competed to see who could race the fastest from one building to another. But our competition waned after the day that Eddie lost control of his hand truck as he sped down the ramp into the cold cup building, launching him into a perfect forward flip ending in a three point landing on the warehouse's cement floor.

As far as I was concerned, I did not need other friends.

Although we lived in our own little world at 59 Freneau Avenue, we were also creatures of the Jersey Shore. The beach towns that hugged the coast were Sloan Products' lifeline, and we spent a tremendous amount of time there. At an early age, we were each able to identify which of the boardwalk shops were our customers, and many evenings and weekends in the summer were spent accompanying my parents on sales calls and last minute deliveries to this mainstay of the family business.

74

When my parents had a free weekend day in the summer, we went to the beach. First Bradley Beach, a Jersey Shore Jewish enclave. Then from 1959 through 1963, we belonged to the Elberon Surf Club, a more exclusive Jewish beachfront. Most summer weekdays, my mother was too busy to take us, so she arranged for her friend Gladys Schwartz to drive the four of us and her two sons to the club in her Cadillac. The six of us squeezed in and hung out the windows as Gladys smoked and talked and drove 80 miles an hour on the back roads from Matawan to Elberon. We played on the beach and swam with the crowd of Jewish children, kids named Benjie or Stevie or Stewie or Shelly or Robin or Allen or Kenny. We rode the waves on Sloan Products' rafts and built sand castles with pails and shovels supplied by my family's business. We made endless trips to the snack bar where we bought pretzel rods (three for a nickel) or frozen Milky Way candy bars, and washed them down with cherry Cokes and ice cream sodas.

At the end of the workday, my mother and Olga joined us at the club. We got dressed up in our cabana and then met my father on the boardwalk in nearby Asbury Park, where he was still calling on customers, and had dinner and strolled up and down with the other nattily attired Jerseyans. We played miniature golf and skee-ball, rode the tilt-a-whirl, and bought salt water taffy and candy apples. On the Fourth of July, we joined the crowd on the boardwalk to watch the fireworks display beyond the Asbury Park convention hall pier. The smoke from the blasts was guaranteed to make Howie and me wheeze.

On weekends, Olga and my parents took us to the club, carrying large baskets full of corned beef sandwiches, peaches, apricots, watermelon, and thermoses of Olga's home-brewed iced tea. Olga held court in front of our cabana while my mother played mah jong with her Jewish contemporaries. My father read pulp fiction on a lounge chair by the pool, his balding pate turning pink.

Whenever we expressed interest in a hobby or activity, Olga or my mother immediately bought us equipment or signed us up for lessons. One summer, Eddie came home from camp talking about archery and a target and a bow and arrows appeared on the lawn within a matter of days. We had golf clubs and guitars and a piano. We had ping pong and pool tables in the basement. We took music and dance and drama and horseback riding lessons. When Sandi expressed an interest in art, she was driven the 45 miles to New York City on Saturday mornings to take drawing lessons at the Museum of Modern Art.

Despite our closeness and shared experience, Howie, Sandi, Eddie, and I each had distinct places in the family pecking order that Olga maintained, and each of us developed our own way to cope with the peculiar nature of life at Sloan Products. Howie demanded constant attention. There were the tantrums, like that night he sat outside in his underwear in a snowstorm because he refused to brush his teeth, and the physical infirmities (and the attendant visits to numerous specialists) resulting from his eczema and asthma. Unlike Sandi, Eddie, or I, he was capable of confronting our grandmother, arguing with her toe to toe. He always took charge of the other three of us, constantly ordering us around, whether making up and enforcing the rules for our wiffle ball games, or, clipboard in hand, acting as a de facto foreman responsible for a Sloan Products' work crew consisting of the other three goonks. Even though Howie was three months younger than Sandi, he was a year ahead of her in school (having skipped second grade). This gave him special status, particularly in Olga's eyes, as both the first born male grandchild and the most advanced in school, where he excelled.

As a child, my brother was obsessed with baseball. Despite his skinny frame, he was a good athlete, a star infielder on his little league teams. He listened constantly to Yankees' games on the radio in our room, keeping score in a spiral notebook he kept in his night table. When he was not doing his school work, he was either dragging me outside to play ball with him, or creating game situations in his head so he could determine in advance what to do in different scenarios.

Sandi was the yin to my brother's yang—sweet, agreeable, and incapable of confronting Olga or anyone else in the house. In many ways, she was most like my mother, never saying no to taking on a task, always willing to pitch in. She bore the brunt of Howie's bossiness, and as Olga's motherless female grandchild, Sandi was often the primary focus of Olga's attention. That meant countless shopping trips to Saks and other upscale stores, but it also meant being in the crosshairs of Olga's scrutiny at all times. Olga wanted Sandi to be a perfect young lady, and in those rare moments when Sandi was less than perfect, merely acting in ways appropriate to her age, Olga became enraged.

Sandi was blond, unlike Howie and I who were dark haired, and perky. She spent her free time playing the piano and singing, practicing show tunes over and over as she sat on the bench just below the portrait of her mother in Olga's living room. At other times, she could be found out on the lawn, doing cartwheels, or shimmying in her room as she listened to "Heat Wave" by Martha and the Vandellas over and over.

Eddie was Olga's poor, motherless youngest grandchild. Sometimes I thought his name was Poor Eddie, since that was how Olga referred to him most of the time. Like Sandi, Eddie avoided confrontation and argument. But he also had the ability to remove himself from the frantic nature of our home, whether through the fantasy world he constructed for his toy soldiers, immersing himself in comic books or "The Lord of the Rings," playing his guitar, piano, and organ, and most noticeably by sitting separately from the rest of us at dinner. Eddie was not beyond taking advantage of the poor, suffering caricature that Olga created for him. He had her wrapped around his finger and, as a result, he was free to do what he wanted.

And then there was me. I was quiet and well-behaved and rarely interacted with Olga. It usually took her three tries before she got my name right. It was as if my name was "Howie, Eddie, Neil."

As much as we were together, I had a special world in which to retreat. Just before I started Fifth Grade, my parents bought Howie and me a set of the World Book Encyclopedia. The red leather bound volumes sat in a small bookcase in the corner of our over-furnished room. They became my special companions. I sat on the floor in front of the case and ran my fingers across the spines of the volumes, stopping on the gold letters of the alphabet that identified the contents of each book, trying to decide which portion I wanted to read on a given day. Soon, I started spending all my free moments there, methodically working my way through the set over the course of that school year.

I read it all, but I had my favorite parts, like the geographical sections that described the world that existed beyond Matawan, the maps and descriptions enabling me to travel the globe without leaving the safety net of my room. But my favorite section was "Ships" in the "S" volume. Ironic as it might seem, given my experience on the Brasil, I became obsessed with this section, reading and re-reading it at every opportunity. Whenever we went into the city, I begged my parents to drive along the docks so I could see what boats were in port. I could identify the steamship companies—Cunard, United States Lines, Moore-McCormick, Holland American, Swedish American, the French Line—by the way the smokestacks were painted, and I reveled in the opportunity to display my knowledge. More often than not, I was told that the docks were out of our way, but I always peered across the river from the New Jersey side as we drove back to Matawan, trying to get a glimpse of the things that I knew more about than anyone in my family.

Chapter Sixteen

Although it was only forty-five miles from New York City, the Matawan of my childhood could have been hundreds of miles away. Many of my grade school classmates had rarely, if ever, been to the city, and few of the town's adult residents commuted to New York for work. Matawan was a working-class community. There were some small factories in the area, but also many fruit and vegetable farms. The main highway through town was called Valley Road; it bisected apple orchards as it wound its way to the corn fields of neighboring towns. The town did not have a country club or a swim club.

The few stores of Matawan's downtown lined Main Street: the Farmers' and Merchants' Bank, Rexall Drugs, Bell Foods, and Western Hardware. There was Vogue Cleaners, owned by my parents' close friend Sam Siegel, and Johnny's Cozy Corner, a luncheonette that served hamburgers and shakes that attracted a constant crowd of teenagers. The library was housed in a small 19th century house across from the post office and police station. Down the hill from Main Street was Lake Matawan into which the waters from our own Gravelly Brook flowed.

The social hub of downtown Matawan was Ryan Brothers, a Sloan Products' customer. It was here that townspeople bought their newspapers, magazines, and cigarettes, and where their children dug change from their pockets to buy candy and comic books. It was where our classmates bought their school supplies, a ritual from which we were excluded since our notebooks, paper, pens, and pencils were all furnished out of our family's inventory. In the center of the store was a self-service coffee maker, the hangout where Matawan's business people, my father among them, gathered in the morning to shoot the breeze.

Once beyond the few blocks of the small business district, Main Street was lined with small Victorian houses, American flags often hanging from the rails of their front porches. A mile from downtown, the street name changed to Freneau Avenue, in honor of the American Revolutionary War poet Philip Freneau, the closest thing Matawan had to a local celebrity. Freneau Avenue became a country highway leading to the county seat of Freehold, seven miles away. Our house was located at 59 Freneau Avenue, just beyond the White Shanty Tavern.

Matawan was a town of churches—Presbyterian, Methodist, Lutheran, Baptist, Episcopal and Roman Catholic. Many of my classmates went to after-school Catechism classes at St. Joseph's, and when they were older, to the St. Joseph's Friday night CYO dances. There was a significant black community in Matawan, most of whom belonged to the Baptist church. But there was no synagogue in town.

Everything about our house and family stood in contrast to the rest of Matawan. Most of the other houses in town were modest in size and situated on small pieces of property. The size of the Sloan Products warehouse dwarfed Matawan's other businesses. When my mother started driving a Cadillac, it was conspicuously grander than the cars that most everyone else in town drove. But being Jewish was what really set us apart.

Until I was in middle school, we were one of only three Jewish families in town. My classmates noticed when I missed school for the Jewish high holidays. They noticed when I was permitted to go home for lunch during Passover. When I answered questions correctly in class, some of the kids whispered "Einstein." One time during a recess game of softball, as a grounder bounced off my glove, my classmate Jackie Johnson screamed "go get it, kike."

For a few years my parents and their circle of Jewish friends in the neighboring town of Keyport were able to sustain a small Jewish congregation there. That is where the four of us started attending Hebrew school, but the temple closed. We then joined Temple Beth Mordecai, a large conservative temple in Perth Amboy, twenty minutes from Matawan.

Once we joined Beth Mordecai, it became the focus of our Saturday and Sunday mornings for years. We attended Hebrew school from 9:00 to 12:00 on Saturday mornings, learning Hebrew and every aspect of the Sabbath liturgy, as well as participating in the weekly children's service. On Sunday mornings, our classes ran from 10:00 to

80

12:00, focusing on Jewish history and culture. My parents drove back and forth between Matawan and Perth Amboy twice on Saturday and twice on Sunday to drop us off and to pick us up, 160 minutes of driving each weekend. And in the months leading up to our respective bar and bat mitzvah's, Cantor Edelstein came to our house one evening a week to teach us the chants for our Torah and Haftorah portions. He always managed to show up around dinner time and got a free meal for his trouble.

My family became central figures at Beth Mordecai. During the High Holidays, we had a row of prime seats right in front of the altar. Olga bought large memorial plaques on the wall honoring her dead relatives, including Charlotte. My mother organized holiday shows, including writing the script for the school's Hanukah presentation. One year she was also President of the Sisterhood. My father served as an officer of the congregation, and Howie and Sandi became officers of United Synagogue Youth. At our bar and bat mitzvahs, we ran the service from start to finish, chanting every Hebrew prayer.

Although my family was dedicated to Beth Mordecai, we still did things the Olga Sloan way. On the High Holidays, my father, Howie, and I arrived for services early in the morning, but Olga always came late, ensuring a grand entrance in front of the whole congregation. After Rosh Hashanah services ended in the early afternoon, Olga had my mother drive her to nearby Millburn or Short Hills to spend the rest of the holy day shopping. When Olga donated new Torah crowns to the temple, she made sure that a special ceremony was planned to acknowledge her generosity.

I had one friend during all my time at Beth Mordecai, a boy named Kenny Isaacson who lived in Perth Amboy within walking distance of the temple. I occasionally went to his house after Hebrew school where we read comic books together and talked about baseball or the girls in our classes. One spring, Kenny's father took the two of us to the Mayor's Trophy game at Shea Stadium, the annual exhibition game between the Yankees and the Mets. Kenny's father was a tall, gaunt man with dark, slicked back hair and a pencil moustache. There was always a cigarette hanging from the corner of his mouth. He drove us in his beat-up station wagon, dark smoke pouring out of the muffler at all times. On the way back to Perth Amboy after the game, we made numerous stops on the shoulder of the New Jersey Turnpike, as Mr. Isaacson added oil to the engine from the box of oil cans he kept in the back of the car. The plan was for me to sleep over at Kenny's house, but something about Kenny's father made me uneasy. Naturally, when we finally made it to Perth Amboy I immediately called my father and had him come and get me. I never did spend the night there.

The centerpiece of our Jewish home life was Passover. It was a huge affair, usually around forty people including all of Olga's cousins and my father's parents and other members of his family. My mother also had an open door policy—anyone who did not have a place to go for Passover was welcome at our Seder.

Rented rectangular tables were lined up in our center hallway to create one long banquet table. For days in advance, Olga, Sadie, Annie, and my mother cleaned and polished the good China, crystal, and silverware. My mother and Olga drove to the lower east side to buy fresh fish at the Essex Street Market and gallons of sweet kosher wine at Shapiro's winery. The house smelled for days as Olga and my mother cleaned, ground, seasoned, and cooked the fish to make their own gefilte fish. They also made huge bowls of beet colored horseradish, and several pots of chicken soup. There was roast beef and roast turkey, potato kugel and asparagus. The big kitchen table was covered with platters of macaroons, egg kichel, and honey cake.

Each year on the night of the Seder, a freckle-faced black woman named Garnet came to help serve and clean up. She hugged and kissed the four of us, always pulling my head to her chest as I blushed in embarrassment. My paternal grandfather Harry conducted the Seder. He sat at one end of the long table and droned on in Hebrew for what seemed like an eternity as most of the crowd ignored him and talked. The children sat at the other end of the table; we felt like we were 100 yards away from my grandfather. But all eyes focused on us as Eddie and I, as the two youngest in attendance, had to chant the four questions for the entire crowd. Hours later, when everyone was finally leaving, Olga and my mother gave out containers of gefilte fish for their guests to take home.

Chapter Seventeen

Fifth grade was a momentous year. Yes, I now had my World Book, but it was also a time of perspective-altering events and family turmoil.

A few days before the school year started, Martin Luther King, Jr. led the march on Washington. Howie and I watched excerpts of the famous "I Have a Dream" speech on the nightly news with my father. Even as a soon to turn ten-year old, I could sense that something momentous was happening.

My teacher that year was Mr. Veaux. He was new to the district, and the first male teacher I ever had. Mr. Veaux was tall and lanky, with a long neck and a pronounced Adam's apple. He looked like Ichabod Crane as described by Washington Irving. For the first time, I saw that it was acceptable for a man to make a living talking about stories and books. Most important for me, since Mr. Veaux was new to the school system, he never had my older brother as a student. In my other years of school, I invariably ended up with a teacher that the overachieving Howie had a few years before. My school year usually began with the teacher saying "If you're just half the student that your brother was, you'll do just fine." In Mr. Veaux's class, I was spared that comparative burden.

Armed with my burgeoning World Book knowledge and the freedom to be judged without being measured against Howie's prior performance, my hand was constantly raised in class, as I was poised to answer almost every question Mr. Veaux asked. But my classmates' whispers of "Einstein" or "Mr. Harvard" or "not again" each time Mr. Veaux called on me started to dissuade me, and after a few months I thought twice before volunteering.

Our house was a whirlwind of activity in the fall of 1963. In addition to the usual focus on Sloan Products, there was a bar and bat mitzvah to plan—a joint event celebrating Howie and Sandi's milestone over the course of the last weekend in December. The event was also unusual. Sandi was one of the first girls to be bat mitzvahed at extremely conservative Beth Mordecai, and the joint ceremony was the first of its kind at our temple. That fall Olga and my mother were consumed with guest lists and seating charts, menu selections and flower arrangements, and, of course, shopping. It seemed like the women of our house had taken up residence at Chez Mode for fittings of the various outfits they were buying. And we all spent even more time than usual at Beth Mordecai, now adding Friday night services to our weekly schedule. All this attention on Howie and Sandi and their star-billing gave me all the more time to dive into my World Book in peace.

On Friday November 22 of that year, I was sitting in Mr. Veaux's classroom when Mrs. Clark, a long-time teacher in Matawan, came into our classroom crying. She told us that President Kennedy had been shot in the head and that there was no information about his condition. A few minutes later, school was dismissed for the day. As we exited the building, many of my classmates were giddy over the prospect of leaving school early. I searched for my cousin Eddie until I remembered that he was home sick, so I walked home alone.

By the time I made it home, President Kennedy had been pronounced dead. Even though it was the middle of a workday afternoon, I came home to find Olga and her sisters sitting at the table in the big kitchen, watching the unfolding events on the small black and white television set in the corner of the room. Like most of the country, everything in our household came to a halt that weekend. There was no discussion of Sloan Products or the bar and bat mitzvah as we were all glued to our televisions watching the historic events of that weekend—the swearing in of LBJ, the arrest of Lee Harvey Oswald, the state funeral in Washington, and Oswald's murder by Jack Ruby. Even Olga and Charlie refrained from fighting.

Within a few days of that weekend, my family's focus returned to business and the last minute preparations for the bar and bat mitzvah, now only a month away. Olga, Sadie, Annie, my mother, and Sandi had closets full of new silk and satin dresses, and my brother his first suit. Eddie and I got new sports jackets for the weekend, matching navy blue blazers with red trim around the collars. We looked like two little lords in waiting.

The celebratory weekend got off to a less than auspicious start. Sandi's father Irving did not show up at the Friday night service at which his daughter was being honored. Sandi was devastated, but her hurt feelings were only made worse when we arrived home. Through the closed door to Irving's apartment, we could hear laughter and female voices.

On the morning of the bar and bat mitzvah service, Sandi and Howie made an incongruous pair as they stood on the bema in Beth Mordecai's large main sanctuary. My brother was short and skinny, less than 5 feet tall and well under 100 pounds. Sandi had just about reached her full height of 5'5", and with her blonde hair teased into a bouffant for the occasion, she looked even taller. She towered over my brother as they faced the congregation. Unlike the previous night, Irving attended this service.

The reception took place the following afternoon, Sunday December 29, 1963, and Irving was again a no-show. The big party started at the same time as the New York Giants-Chicago Bears NFL championship game. I spent most of the afternoon huddled in the catering hall men's room with the Sloan Products' business contacts and most of the other male guests, trying to watch the game on the attendant's small black and white TV.

As 1963 ended and 1964 began, my siblings and I were swept up by a new phenomenon—the British rock and roll invasion and the Beatles first trip to the U.S. The four of us crowded into my room to listen to "Meet the Beatles" over and over, using tennis rackets as make-believe guitars as we gyrated along to the music. Rock and roll started to blare from our room at all hours, as Howie and I listened to stacks of 45's or top 40 radio on WMCA, home of the "Good Guys."

The night that the Beatles made their first appearance on the Ed Sullivan show, Howie, Sandi, Eddie, and I gathered in front of the TV in my parents' bedroom, anxiously awaiting our heroes' performance. When they started to play and the young female members of the audience started to scream, my father just sat there and shook his head.

Sloan Products took advantage of the moment, adding a number of Beatles related items to the inventory. I took advantage, too, as I convinced my mother to let me have a box of samples of souvenir Beatles pins, each shaped like a guitar with a photo of one of the members of the group. I took them to school and passed them out to the kids in Mr. Veaux's class, making sure to give the Paul pins to the girls in my class.

The spring of 1964 also brought the world to our doorstep, as the World's Fair opened in Flushing Meadow in Queens. My parents, and especially my mother, became huge fans of the fair, and we went often. It was as if my mother used the fair to satisfy her urge to tour the world, as well as to escape the heightened household tension resulting from Olga's confrontations with Irving and Charlie. We visited all the international exhibits, and my mother always made a point of stopping in the International Plaza to sample foreign cuisine on each of our trips. Like my mother, I got caught up in the promise of the future that the fair presented. I could not get enough of it.

The World's Fair also captured the imagination of my classmates, as our school organized an ambitious class trip to the fair for the entire 5th grade. This was a big deal for our small town, as many of my classmates rarely, if ever, went to the city. Our large group gathered early at the Matawan train station. We took the train to Penn Station in Manhattan, where we switched to the Long Island Railroad to Flushing Meadow. We were split into groups of five for the day, with each group supervised by a parent-chaperone. My mother was in charge of my group of five boys. The other boys in my group were more interested in buying souvenirs than in any of the pavilions we toured (with the exception of the Ford pavilion, where we got to sit in Mustang convertibles as part of the Ford ride through history), and we returned to Matawan that evening laden with our purchases. Especially popular were felt Fedoras with large feathers on which we each got our name embroidered. As we stepped off the train, looking like some bizarre Tyrolean oompah band in our odd looking new hats, little Matawan seemed light years removed from the marvels we had just witnessed in Queens.

My year in 5th grade opened my eyes to the possibilities of a life beyond Matawan. The places that I read about in the World Book or saw displayed at the World's Fair, and the music recorded in Liverpool and

86

London that now played non-stop in my room, beckoned. I was only 10 years old, but I had started to think about finding a way to conquer my fear of moving beyond the end of the long driveway at 59 Freneau Avenue.

That spring, Olga and my mother decided the four of us should go to camp. My mother identified a place called Camp Northwood through an ad in the New York Times. It was probably the camp's slogan "Camp Northwood in the pollen free Adirondacks" that attracted her to a place for her allergy prone sons. The camp owner, Harry Pertz, came to Matawan to make his sales pitch. His Yiddish accent sold Olga the minute he walked in the door, but even so Harry proceeded with his complete sales pitch and slide show. He laid it on thick for Olga, pointing out that the meals at camp were "Kosher style," and that Shabbat services were conducted most Friday evenings. The photos we sat and watched in my parents' living room included images of a track meet at Northwood's large athletic field. I was intrigued. I thought that I was a fast runner, but I was always hesitant to compete against my Matawan classmates during recess. Camp might not be such a bad idea after all.

Notwithstanding Harry's persuasive presentation and Olga's positive reaction, my parents decided we needed to check out Camp Northwood. One Saturday that April, we made the eleven hour round-trip drive to Remsen, New York in the same day. Northwood was still covered with snow, so we trudged around the camp as our feet and ankles got soaked. Even when blanketed with snow, the ball field, basketball courts, and lakefront captured our attention. We were sold.

As with everything else, we were not your typical campers. We went to Saks Fifth Avenue to buy our camping gear, and while most campers packed their belongings into small foot-locker sized trunks, Olga bought each of us a steamer-sized trunk big enough to house a small family. We each had a large supply of camp T-shirts emblazoned with the "pollen free" Camp Northwood motto on the front. As summer approached, I knew that sleep-away camp would be a true test for me. Would I be able to confront my anxieties and make it through an entire summer away from home?

Chapter Eighteen

My year in fifth grade also opened another chapter in the struggle between Olga and her former son-in-law Irving. In February, 1964, Irving made a rare appearance one evening in the large kitchen to speak with Olga.

"Olga, I thought I should let you know that I am getting married. I would like to have my wife move into my apartment so I can keep living here."

"You're getting married? What's her name? Who is she and where does she come from, where are her people from?"

"When you meet her you can ask her."

"What the hell are you talking about? You think I'm just going to let some stranger move into my house, sleep in my daughter's bed? You must be out of your mind."

"I would appreciate it if you would think it over."

"Don't hold your breath."

About a week later, Irving appeared in Olga's bedroom and demanded an answer to his request.

"Olga, I need to know if you are going to allow my wife to move in. Have you decided?"

"Didn't you understand what I told you? There is no way in hell that I am going to allow another woman to live in my daughter's apartment."

"I thought that is what you would say, because everything is always about you. I've suffered too, you know. Well, I'll have to find another place to live, and when I do, I want Sandi and Eddie to come live with me."

"Go to hell."

"They're my children, I'm their father. I have every right to have them come live with me."

"Listen to me, you son of a bitch. I never should have let you marry my daughter. Someone like her deserved better than a good-for-nothing like you. And Charlotte was never sick a day in her life until you came along, infecting her with the cancer. Then you run around and act like you don't even have children, and now you've found some floozy because you can't keep a lock on your zipper. Get out of my house, you bastard. You stay away from those children."

"I figured you would try and keep them from me. I'm completely within my rights."

"You'll never get your hands on those children."

Irving stormed out of Olga's room, returned to his apartment, and slammed the door shut. He locked the entrance, and sealed the door with heavy tape. Two weeks later he opened the door and called in Sandi and Eddie, the first time he had seen them in weeks. Irving told them that he was getting married the next day, but they could not come to the wedding. When they started to cry, he made no attempt to comfort them.

Two days later, a moving van drove up to the outside entrance to Irving's apartment. Irving took everything— furniture (some of which belonged to Olga), his belongings, Charlotte's belongings, family photos, the telephone, everything right down to the outlet covers from the wall sockets. Even though Sandi and Eddie were home that afternoon, Irving did not say a word to them. He moved to a small apartment in Matawan, where he lived with his new wife, a tall, dark-haired woman named Pearl. The apartment that Irving had occupied in our house, and which had been his family's home until Charlotte's death, was never occupied again. From that point on it was simply referred to as the "Other Apartment."

The first time Olga and Pearl met was a few weeks later at Beth Mordecai in Perth Amboy. Our whole family was there to watch Eddie lead a Saturday morning service. Irving and Pearl showed up, too. Irving brought Pearl over to Olga and introduced her. Pearl said "Is this what you call a service? In New York we do it much nicer."

Later that spring, Sandi was confirmed at Beth Mordecai. She tried to call Irving several times to invite him to the confirmation ceremony, but she never reached him, so instead she mailed him two tickets. The day of the confirmation, Irving and Pearl arrived after the services had already begun. Afterwards, Irving approached Olga outside the temple to congratulate her.

"Irving, I told you not to talk to her," Pearl screamed. "Spit in her stupid face. Can't you see she has a twisted mind?"

Pearl then turned to Olga. "You think just because you have money and that big house that you can push Irving around, but you're going to get what you have coming to you."

"Get out of my way," Olga yelled back at Pearl.

The confrontation continued in full view of our entire family and many of the members of the congregation, including a close family friend, Seymour Kleinberg, a municipal court judge. Everyone was yelling--my mother telling Pearl to stop screaming at Olga, Irving telling my mother to shut up, my father telling Irving not to tell my mother to shut up--until Judge Kleinberg was finally able to break things up. I was mortified that this was my family.

Shortly after this episode, Irving sent a letter to my mother laying out his view of the situation:

"I would like to set forth in writing what I have told you and your mother prior to my marriage.

"I want you to know that it was always my intention, and still is, for Sandi and Eddie to live with me and my new wife, where they belong, and where they can best mature and develop. I have a very adequate home and a capable wife who can guide the children properly. I know that you and your mother are so busy in the business that you cannot give the children the attention they need.

"Unfortunately, you and your mother made it impossible for me to take the children with me at the time of my marriage and so I allowed them to stay with you 'for the time being' provided that I received your complete cooperation with regard to seeing that the children spend time with me. You have not encouraged the children to visit me and have

90

prevented them from so doing with the constant heavy schedule which you have provided them against my wishes. I want you to know that this cannot and will not continue.

"Helen, you are a mother. Why don't you make some effort to encourage the children to spend a little time with their father? After all, I have been your brother-in-law for many years—living under the same roof—and you act as though I were a perfect stranger. And your mother, an experienced successful businesswoman—who has suffered a great tragedy—has she no regard for another human being?

"I am ready at any time to meet with you and your mother to settle all our difficulties and if we all remain calm perhaps we can come to an arrangement that is satisfactory to all."

A few days later, Judge Kleinberg arranged a meeting among Olga, my parents, Irving, Pearl, and our Rabbi. At the meeting, Pearl insisted that Sandi and Eddie had to come live with Irving and her, even if it meant they had to give up some of their "extravagant activities." Olga told Pearl that Sandi would rather drown herself than live with her father, to which Pearl replied, "If she wants to go drown herself, then let her go drown herself." Whenever Irving tried to speak, Pearl told him to shut up. Nothing was accomplished at the meeting other than to confirm Olga's disdain for Irving and to vault Pearl to the top of Olga's enemies list.

For me, the whole situation added to my general state of uneasiness. The possibility that two of the four goonks might be wrested away from my little world, however remote, was one more thing for me to worry about.

Chapter Nineteen

The last day of school was always special. The four of us would play wiffle ball on the lawn or spud in the driveway until the light had completely faded, the long days of summer at the Jersey Shore stretching before us. But the end of my year in fifth grade in June 1964 was different, and not just because we were leaving in a few days for eight weeks at Camp Northwood. This year on that first night of no homework and no prescribed bedtime, Olga played poker with us.

It was unusual for Olga to engage in any of our childhood activities. She did not read to us or play games. She did not draw or color with us. When we went to the beach, she did not help us build sandcastles and if she went in the water at all, it was a big production that required my mother's assistance at every juncture. She did not bake cookies or cakes. Olga did none of the things we imagined an average grandmother did with her grandchildren. Indeed, she told us often that she was not like any other grandmother we knew. She was right.

But Olga knew how to play cards. For a time, she played in a regular poker game with Gussie Bell, owner of Matawan's downtown grocery store Bell Foods, and some of the other business owners in town. On this one night in late June 1964, she sat with her four grandchildren at the table in the big kitchen and played poker with us. She distributed chips which came straight out of the Sloan Products inventory and shuffled the deck with her stubby fingers, and proceeded to teach us how to play.

"The first thing you need to know is which hands beat others. The best is a straight flush, five cards of the same suit in order—ten, jack, queen, king, ace—then four of a kind, a full house, a flush, a straight, three of a kind, two pair, one pair. I'll show you as we go."

"I already know that. I know how to play," said Howie.

"Well, you'll just have to listen while I show the others."

"What do we do with the chips?" Eddie asked.

"That's for betting. Before each hand you have to ante. That's putting a chip in the pot so you are entitled to play that hand. Each chip stands for some money, say a nickel or a dime or a quarter. Then there are rounds of betting. You have to decide if you have a good hand and want to bet or a lousy hand and want to fold—that means drop out of that round. I'll explain that as we go along, too. But the most important thing to learn is how to bluff."

"What's bluffing?" asked Sandi.

"Well, you are not always going to have a good hand. But you can still win if you can make the other players think you have such a good hand that they decide to fold. That's bluffing. You have to keep the same expression on your face no matter if you have a good hand or a bad hand, so the other players can't tell. It's like when I'm hondling in a store—I can't let the store owner know what I'm really willing to pay. I have to make him think that I'll walk away if he doesn't drop the price."

"Isn't that sort of cheating?" I asked.

"No, Howie...Eddie...I mean Neil. You have to learn to get the upper hand on people, to take advantage of opportunities. That's an important lesson in life, not only in poker. Other grandmothers don't teach their grandchildren important things like this, certainly not your Grandma Lena. You're lucky to have a grandmother with a head for business."

That was the only time I remember her playing poker with us. It was as if Olga felt it was a piece of education we each needed before we went off to camp.

Chapter Twenty

On the morning of July 1, 1964, my parents and Olga drove the four of us to Grand Central Station where the Northwood campers gathered to board the train for the long ride to Utica, New York, the nearest station to the camp's site in the small town of Remsen. We were each dressed in our navy blue Northwood t-shirts and regulation camp shorts. Our large trunks had already been shipped ahead; all that we carried were the shoeboxes my mother had packed for each of us, containing a large lunch and a pad of MadLibs to play on the train with our new friends.

As we entered the station's vast waiting room, hundreds of campers came into view. Numerous camps departed from Grand Central in those days, and noisy campers were gathering under the signs for their respective summer destinations. As we approached the Northwood banner, my heart started to pound. My parents checked us in with a counselor carrying a large clipboard, and soon it was time to board the train. Eddie and I sat together, our shoeboxes nestled in our laps. I stared out the window and hardly spoke for the entire ride.

When we arrived in Utica, we were met at the station by more Northwood counselors who shepherded us onto yellow school buses for the 30 minute ride to camp. When we pulled into the camp's long gravel drive, Harry Pertz, his wife Sylvia, and the rest of the camp staff were waiting, smiling and waving to their summer charges.

Northwood was a beautiful place. The property started as a hunting lodge, with log cabins disbursed around the large pine-forested property. The gravel drive bisected the camp, with the cabins for the girl campers on one side and the boys' cabins on the other. The buildings were set on a bluff looking over pristine Hinckley Lake, eleven miles long and a mile wide with a pine covered island in the middle.

My first few days at Northwood were tough for me, especially trying to sleep in a cabin with twelve other boys and three counselors. I could not resist the temptation to seek relief from my parents. I wrote anguished letters home. My mother's favorite, which she has kept to this day, read: "I hate this place. The food stinks, the lake is polluted, and everyone has diarrhea. Please come get me." When my parents got this letter, they called Howie at camp. To his credit, he told them that I was fine and they should just let me be. It was the best thing he ever did for me.

It turned out that I was well-suited for camp, particularly one populated by kids who were more accepting of me than most of my Matawan classmates. All of the things that differentiated me from other kids in Matawan, especially how my family lived and worked together, were unknown to my Northwood peers. I felt for the first time that I was being judged solely for who I was, not from where I came.

The camp rules regarding cabin cleanliness and chores also appealed to my orderly sensibilities. I learned to canoe, sail, and water ski. I played never-ending games of poker and hearts, knucks and casino, pitch and bridge. I acted and sang in camp shows. But most importantly, I learned to be at ease with myself. I talked incessantly with my new friends. I laughed until tears streamed down my face. I found out that I was witty and could make others laugh. When we had "College Bowl" night, an academic and trivia based quiz competition, no one made fun of me or whispered about me or called me Einstein when I answered the most questions.

Northwood was the site of my life's crowning athletic achievement. Each summer, the last week of camp was devoted to Color War. The camp was divided into two teams for a series of competitive events—all types of sports, whacky relay races, and a camp "sing" during which the teams had to perform three categories of songs (a fight song, a comedy song, and an alma mater about Northwood). During Color War of my second summer at Northwood, when I was eleven, there was a track meet, just like the one Harry Pertz had shown us during the slide show we watched in my parents' living room. The concluding event for the boys of my age group was a one lap race around the camp's ball field, a distance of about 300 yards. I had been listening all summer to David

Shapiro, one of the boys in my cabin, brag about how fast he was and how no one in camp could beat him in a race. As we approached the starting line, I made sure to line up next to David. At the start of the race, he bolted into the lead, but I stayed right at his shoulder. He could not shake me as we made the first and second turns. When we made the final turn into the homestretch, I accelerated past him and won easily. I smoked him. My Color War teammates cheered wildly as they gathered around me and pounded me on the back. Just as I suspected, I was fast. I proved it to myself that day, which was far more significant than proving it to David Shapiro.

Not everything Harry Pertz said in his sales pitch to Olga turned out to be true. There were no Friday night services. And the "Kosher style" food was not entirely accurate, either. Every day at lunch, a platter of cold cuts, cheese included, was placed on each table as an alternative to whatever hot meal was being served. One day, the deli platters included ham, something that was never served in our house. My brother grabbed the platter from his group's table and marched with righteous indignation to the staff table where the Pertz family sat. "I thought this was a Kosher style camp" said Howie to Harry Pertz. Ham made no further appearances during our Northwood years, although I must admit that I was curious to try some to see what all the fuss was about.

While we were at camp, my mother wrote letters to each of us every night, and she was constantly sending us care packages full of candy and snacks, as well as small toys from Sloan Products. On visiting weekend, my parents and Olga and our dog Taffy arrived after their five hour drive with boxes of food, not just candy and snacks but also salami and rye bread. Olga strolled through the bucolic mountain setting wearing a dress and orthopedic shoes and plenty of costume jewelry, her handbag always draped over her wrist. On the last day of camp, my parents made the long drive to pick up our oversized trunks rather than have them shipped home like all the other campers did. We took the train back to the city with our camp friends where my parents were waiting. I never did figure out how they did all that driving and still beat us to Grand Central Terminal.

I had my first kiss at Northwood, with a girl named Judy Beim in the bushes that lined the drive that separated the girls and boys' sides of the camp. I made close friends, an inseparable trio of Arnie Engelman of Greenwich Village, Dan Saltman of Akron, Ohio, and myself. And, for the first time in my life, I had complete and unabashed fun. I ran with abandon during games of Capture the Flag. Engelman, Saltman, my other bunk mates, and I became amateur pyromaniacs, conducting experiments in the large fieldstone fireplace in our cabin. Our studies came to an abrupt end when we poured water into a pot of melted crayons, sending a soaring flame to the ceiling of the cabin as we all ran out the door screaming. Engelman, Saltman, and I then focused our energy on more benign activities, such as the rest time show we hosted on the camp's own radio station, W.O.O.D.

It seemed like I spent all my days at Northwood laughing. Saltman was particularly adept at working me up to a state of hysteria at "lights out," when we were supposed to be lying quietly in our beds. Our counselor one summer was a young man named Larry Lichter. He was in a bad mood the entire season, often hung over, and his attitude towards us was not improved by the constant jokes we made about his name ("Fred walked over and kissed the girl, but Larry Lichter.") One night when he was especially cranky, Saltman kept whispering puns in my ear. As I laughed uncontrollably, Lichter pulled a large knife out of the duffle bag beneath his bed. He wielded it above his head as he towered over me, asking "What's so funny?" I continued to giggle as I pointed at Saltman. Lichter went into the bathroom, emerged with a wet roll of toilet paper, and wrapped Dan's head like a mummy.

Other counselors were more endearing. Tony "AC" Cuda introduced us to R&B music and taught us how to dance the "Funky Broadway." At one of our annual camp trips to the Booneville County Fair, our counselor Paul Sheldon slipped five dollars to a roustabout so he would not let Engelman and me get off a Ferris wheel. And one night, our counselor Ken Turow lay on his bunk, waxing philosophic: "Someday you guys will realize that this was the best time of your life, the only time when you were completely carefree and without responsibility. Don't take it for granted." He was right.

Northwood was the first place where I exhibited leadership skills. Camp also awakened the activist inside of me, as we sang antiwar and civil rights songs and listened to our counselors talk about Martin Luther King and Malcolm X, LBJ and Vietnam, Phil Ochs and Bob Dylan. I was all the things that life in Matawan had inhibited me from becoming. Learning to transfer these newly discovered attributes to my world at Sloan Products was still to be a long work in process.

Chapter Twenty-One

When we returned to Matawan after our first summer at Northwood, our daily routines remained much the same as they had been my entire life. My parents still got up incredibly early. My mother made my father breakfast, usually poached eggs and toast, which he ate while drinking what looked like a bowl full of coffee and reading the morning paper. (We were a newspaper-reading household. On any given day we had copies of the Daily News, the Times, the Post, the Journal-American, the Herald Tribune, the Wall Street Journal, the Asbury Park Press, the Red Bank Register, and our hometown weekly, the Matawan Journal.) Helen then headed to the front of the house to tend to Olga, help her into her corset, and go over their plans and schedule for the day. By that time, Sadie and Annie were sitting in the large kitchen, eating pot cheese or herring or Wheatina, drinking tea or Ovaltine. Charlie was either eating in his room or, if it was fall, outside raking leaves. I don't remember Olga and her brother and sisters ever exchanging morning pleasantries—no "good morning" or "how are you today?" or "how are you feeling?" Morning was just the time they got ready to walk down the back stairs and go to the office. Most mornings, Charlie avoided Olga, deferring the continuation of their latest battle until both were at work.

My brother and I awoke to our clock radio each morning, the Charlie O'Brien and Benny show, part of the WMCA Good Guys top 40 AM radio schedule. We straggled into the kitchen with barely enough time for Howie to consume the egg nog and toast my mother made for him each day, part of her attempt to fatten his thin frame. I almost never ate breakfast. Four brown paper lunch bags with our names written on them were lined up on the counter, ready for us to take to school. Sometimes Eddie and I mistakenly took the other's bag, and we would have to find each other at lunchtime to effect a trade—he was not interested in my corned beef and I could not stomach his bologna.

My mother drove the four of us to school—either the 1.5 miles to the Broad Street Elementary School or the two miles to the new high school/junior high school building on Atlantic Avenue. My father stopped briefly in the office to gather catalogues before getting in his car for the day, often making a quick detour to Ryan Brothers for more coffee and some local chit chat as he headed out to start calling on his customers.

When my mother returned, her day of work began in earnest. She finalized the truck routes for the day's deliveries and supervised the loading of the trucks. Sadie performed her final bill extensions. Annie worked on additional orders or re-stocked the shelves behind the packing table. Once Olga and Charlie both arrived in the office, it did not take much for the day's battle to begin. Sometimes they started in at each other immediately. Other days, each would pretend to ignore the other while surreptitiously eavesdropping to see what the other was saying and doing. Olga told Charlie to get off his ass and go do some selling. Charlie complained that Olga deliberately undercut him by failing to stock the kind of merchandise that his customers wanted. Olga countered that Charlie's customers did not pay their bills and that he should stop freeloading off her and go back to his wife. The only respite was around mid-morning, when Charlie finally decided to go out on the road to call on customers or to drive around Matawan trawling for cheap day laborers.

All day there was a steady flow of cars and trucks, the bell in the house connected to the hose on the driveway constantly signaling the arrivals and departures. There were deliveries of merchandise, pick-ups by UPS, salesman calling to ply their wares, and customers who either wanted to meet with Olga and my mother in the showroom or who preferred to pick up their small orders rather than have them delivered. Annie or my mother made several trips into town over the course of the day, to pick up the mail from our large P.O. box at Matawan's post office, or to make deposits and withdrawals at the Farmers' and Merchants' Bank.

The office phone lines rang all day, too—customers placing orders, salesman or manufacturer's representatives who wanted to speak to Olga or my mother, my father checking in from the road. The bell ringing was punctuated by the constant blare of the office intercom system, the shrill voices of Olga, Sadie, or Annie barking their commands throughout the warehouse.

Sloan Products closed for lunch, but Olga, Sadie, or Annie still answered the business phone extension in the kitchen while they ate. My mother usually spent her lunch hour either performing errands in town or starting the preparation for that night's dinner. If Charlie was home at lunchtime, he and Olga made sure to exchange a few verbal jabs.

At the end of our school day, my mother made the rounds to pick the four of us up, although if she was busy we walked home. If we did not have any after school activities, once we got home we threw down our books, had a snack, and reported for duty in the office to help out before we started our homework.

Late in the day the trucks returned from their delivery routes. My mother collected the drivers' delivery receipts and any payments they received for C.O.D. orders. She then turned her attention to dinner. By this time, Charlie had returned from his meanderings and the nightly pyrotechnics began. We ate our dinner and tried to ignore the gathering storm, but it usually found us, often following us to our rooms as we were trying to do our homework.

My father dragged himself home after his long day on the road and my mother struggled to stay awake as she did her work.

This is how it was every work day I lived at 59 Freneau Avenue.

Within the contours of these daily routines, however, were subtle variations, which were generally dependent on Olga's mood and whims. My mother's schedule, for example, was always dependent on Olga's demands: drive Olga to the Lower East Side to buy the dried mushrooms she used to make mushroom barley soup, or to visit her optician on East Broadway when she needed new glasses; drive Olga to the Upper West Side to get fitted for a new corset; drive Olga to banks spread throughout central New Jersey so she could get her monthly interest posted in the passbooks for her numerous savings accounts; drive Olga to a car or truck dealership so she could hondle over the price for a new vehicle for the business; drive Olga to Millburn or Short Hills where she would make the rounds at Saks, Bloomingdale's, and Chez Mode. Whatever the errand,

Olga always had her purse hanging from her wrist, a thick wad of cash tucked inside at the ready. Olga only paid in cash.

On her shopping trips with my mother, Olga rarely bought anything without first attempting to knock down the price. When shopping for jewelry, she would ask to see a ring or a necklace or earrings, handle the piece for several minutes, and then ask "how much?" When she was told the price, she would drop the piece in disgust, state it was worthless, and stomp off, only to return a minute later offering half the asking price. This exercise would be repeated until Olga got an acceptable discount. Any shopping trip that allowed her to browbeat a salesperson was a success.

Even at night, Olga's presence permeated the entire household. From her room at the front of the house, she paced up and down the long center hall at all hours, most often to talk to my mother about some aspect of the business or some task she wanted my mother to perform. It was not unusual to find Olga in the large kitchen at 2:00 or 3:00 in the morning, scrubbing pots or making large batches of iced tea. Sometimes late at night she scanned the Sloan Products' master ledger that my mother maintained to see how much money my father's customers and Charlie's customers owed the business, usually yelling "Who's crazy here?" when she saw how much credit had been extended. Other nights she could be heard wandering the house, singing the refrain from "Sunrise Sunset" over and over. On Saturday nights, she could always be found in her room, never wanting to miss a moment of Lawrence Welk.

For us goonks, our daily life varied because of the different types of interactions we had with the other members of the household. Howie was always eager to engage the adults in conversation, from mundane daily matters to sports to political debate, particularly about the Vietnam War. Howie and Sandi also were involved in so many activities—drama school; scouts; Howie's baseball, wrestling, and golf; Sandi's dancing, piano lessons, and art classes; United Synagogue Youth; and student council—that they spent extra time with my mother, who was responsible for their comings and goings.

After Charlotte's death, Sandi bore the brunt of much of Olga's attention. Olga was consumed with outfitting Sandi in clothes from the

102

finest department stores, and expected Sandi to behave like the princess that her wardrobe befitted. As a result, Sandi was a regular participant in the shopping trips for which my mother chauffeured Olga. Sandi also had the most contact with Sadie and Annie, since she shared a room with Sadie and lived adjacent to Annie and Olga.

Sandi and Eddie had a special bond as a result of what they went through with their mother's death and their father's negligence. But unlike Sandi, who threw herself into as many activities as she could fit in a day (the Helen Selinger model), Eddie retreated into his own little world. First, it was his toy soldier collection. He would line them up on the edge of his bathtub and knock them into the water one by one. Later, it was comic books. Eddie was a superhero fan—Superman, Batman, Aquaman, and the Green Lantern (I preferred more lighthearted fare—Archie and Richie Rich). Finally, it was a combination of "The Lord of the Rings" and his music (piano, organ, and guitar).

Eddie and my brother rarely spent time alone together, probably because Eddie had little interest in sports. Eddie grudgingly played in many of the endless ball games that Howie and I constructed on the lawn or in our room, but we always had to cajole him into participating. For me, it was different, perhaps because Eddie and I were so close in age, or maybe because we shared a similar attitude about the goings on in our house which we both viewed as something to be avoided whenever possible. Yet, while I could be successful at disappearing from the fray without being noticed, Eddie was the subject of Olga's constant refrain: "Where's Eddie?" She needed to know at all times where he was and what was he doing. This became a running joke among the four goonks, asking each other constantly "Where's Eddie?" even if he was right there with us. For me though, the joke was bittersweet. No one in my house asked "Where's Neil?"

At any rate, I was allowed access into Eddie's world in a way that Sandi and Howie were not. I was permitted to join him in his toy soldier exercises. We played Stratego and Risk. We watched countless old movies together, mainly swashbucklers and science fiction; the "Flame and the Arrow" and "Forbidden Planet" were two of our favorites. We traveled back and forth to school together. And we always worked side by side in the office, either laboring under Annie's glare, or following Sam around the warehouse like two groupies stalking a rock star.

My relationship with my brother was totally different, as so much of it focused on sports. Like our father, we were Yankees fans. We would lie in our beds at night, listening to games on the radio. Our father took us to baseball, football, basketball, and hockey games. We invented a game called "bed football," the object of which was to get from one side of our adjoining beds to the other without being tackled. We wrestled. We rolled our socks into balls and shot them at the metal wastebasket we used as a doorstop.

We also sat at the desks in our crowded room, dutifully doing our homework. And we fought like brothers do. One evening I was sitting astride his chest, holding a pillow over his face. Just as I asked, "Are you dead yet?" my father happened to walk into our room. He grabbed me by the collar and yanked me off Howie, as he barked at me "Don't ever let me hear you talking like that to your brother again."

I treasured order and neatness; Howie was a slob and it drove me crazy. I could not fall asleep unless all the drawers in the room were closed. A soon as I got in bed, Howie would walk around the room, opening each drawer an inch or so, and then watched with glee until I could not take it any more and jumped out of bed to shut them all. When Howie was a teenager and started staying out late on Saturday nights, he would come into our room, turn on the lights, and yell "Neil, it's time to get up for school." I fell for it every time, staggering around looking for my clothes while I asked "Why is it so dark?" until Howie collapsed on the floor laughing.

Like Eddie and me, Howie and Sandi spent a great deal of time together due to their closeness in age. The difference was that Howie bossed Sandi around, and she never pushed back. Sandi and I were more alike, non-confrontational. I liked to sit on the floor in her room and listen to records with her or watch musicals on Million Dollar Movie. The problem was that to get to the room that Sandi shared with Sadie, or to Eddie's room, I had to walk by Olga's room. This was a major deterrent to my visiting that end of the house, since there was always the risk that I might catch a glimpse of Olga in her corset or, worse, one of her sheer nightgowns. How Sandi and Eddie lived amidst that constant threat was a mystery to me.

Chapter Twenty-Two

The confidence that I gained at Camp Northwood in the summer of 1964 did not enhance my experience in 6th grade, the 1964-1965 school year. It was an odd year, my last at the Broad Street Elementary School, a combination of an academic vacuum and the closing chapter of the struggle between Olga and Irving to wrest control of Sandi and Eddie's lives.

My 6th grade teacher was named Mr. Bragdon, another new teacher in our system. Mr. Bragdon displayed the characteristics of a mid 1960's swinging bachelor; he even looked a little like Rock Hudson, straight out of a movie with Doris Day with his chiseled features, thick black hair, dark suits, crisp white shirts, and narrow ties. Each morning, he screeched into the school parking lot in his red MG roadster convertible. When he arrived in the classroom, he proceeded to transcribe crossword puzzles from the morning newspaper onto the blackboard. He then told us to work together to solve the puzzle as he sat at his desk, putting his head down on the surface and napping. My classmates relied on me to work on the crossword assignment as they made paper airplanes, shot spitballs, and generally went wild until our teacher finally woke up and started the day's lessons.

When he was awake and focused, Mr. Bragdon had us work on ambitious class-wide projects. We were studying the geography of Africa that year, so Mr. Bragdon had us paint a large map of the continent on a board about six feet high and three feet wide. The countries were painted in bright colors, but without any identifying names; a nail was hammered into the center of each country, protruding to the back side of the board. Along one side of the board, the name of each African nation was listed in black paint, with a nail hammered into the board just to the left of the name. Mr. Bragdon then connected wires on the back between the country name and the corresponding place on the map. Also on the front were two wires attached to a battery and a small light bulb at one end. If the end of one wire was placed upon the nail next to a nation name, while the end of the other wire was placed upon the nail in the corresponding place on the map, a complete circuit was created and the bulb lit.

The point, of course, was to use the map to teach the class the names and locations of all the countries in Africa. Mr. Bragdon held a wire to a place on the map and asked a student to hold the other wire to the name of the country. That year, there were twin black sisters in my class, Charmaine and Jarmaine Williams. While Mr. Bragdon held the wire to the nail located in the middle of the map of Niger, he asked Jarmaine (or was it Charmaine?) to identify the name of the country. "That's Nigger," she replied. "It's right next to Nigger-ia," she added, pointing to Nigeria. She did not seem to understand why her teacher and classmates were laughing.

I had no real friends in that class, and I spent much of the day pining for my Northwood buddies and daydreaming about what the distant summer of 1965 held in store. Mr. Bragdon played softball with us each day at recess, but with the absence of any real comrades, I lost whatever confidence about my athletic abilities I had gained over the prior summer. When I came to bat, all I could think about was getting it over with as quickly as possible. Let's just say I went 0 for the 6th grade.

Late that fall, Mr. Bragdon was in a bad car accident. His MG flipped over and he broke his leg and several ribs, and punctured a lung. He was absent for weeks, and a series of substitute teachers took over our class. When he returned, Mr. Bragdon had a dark beard and was using crutches. He had even less energy and focus for teaching. The crossword puzzles returned. The class ran amok.

Also that fall, in November 1964, Irving sued for custody of his children, naming as defendants Olga, my parents, Sadie, Annie, and Charlie. The case became the central focus of our world. Olga's usual agitated state was pushed to new extremes.

Olga called her friend Judge Seymour Kleinberg for advice. He referred Olga to a suave and elegant looking lawyer named Bob Friedlander. He was tall and thin with a mane of white hair, always nattily attired in suit and tie. Friedlander did not usually handle custody cases; he

107

was primarily a bankruptcy attorney. But the recommendation of a Jewish judge mattered more to Olga than experience. She hired Friedlander for the case.

Friedlander came to the house often to prepare for the trial, but my brother and I were kept on the outside of the process. The adults talked constantly about the case, but if I was around the conversation either stopped or continued in Yiddish. But nothing stopped Olga from her incessant cursing about Irving and what a bastard he was, how he had killed her daughter, and what a bitch he had married.

In preparation for the trial, Friedlander had Olga, each of my parents, Sadie, Annie, and Charlie sign affidavits recounting their versions of Irving's shortcomings as a parent, which they re-iterated in their testimony at the trial. There were also affidavits signed by our school principal, family doctors, and Harry Pertz, owner of Camp Northwood, all to the effect that their only dealings regarding Sandi and Eddie were either with Olga or my mother, never with Irving. The most ironic spin of the facts was in Sadie's affidavit:

"Being raised under [Olga's] care, the children cannot help but absorb some of [her] prestige. The adage of learning by example certainly applies here. The children have learned from her to accept their responsibilities as members of the community. They have learned integrity and high moral principles. They have learned how to talk easily to people, how to be gracious and tactful, and to be interested and considerate of others."

Olga put on an inspired performance when she testified at the trial. It was the complete "Story of O," as she recounted her personal hardships, her success at building Sloan Products after her husband and father died, and her pain in losing her daughter. She listed in detail all the advantages which she provided her grandchildren, noting at every opportunity how Irving contributed nothing for his children's welfare. But the real art of it was the way she maintained her composure, sitting erect in the witness chair without even a hint of her temper and fiery disposition, or the complete disdain she had for Irving and Pearl. The lessons she gave us about bluffing in poker or any other aspect of life were on full display.

108

Also during the trial, Sandi and Eddie were required to meet with the judge in his chambers, outside the presence of Olga, Irving and Pearl. They each told the judge that they wished to continue living with us. The case was fully submitted to the judge for his decision early in the winter of 1965.

In the midst of this tumult, in February of 1965, my parents let me miss almost a month of school. Still buoyed from the cruise on the Brasil three years earlier, Olga and her sisters booked a two week Caribbean cruise on the sister ship, the S.S. Argentina. Eddie and I went, too. We shared a room with Olga, while Sadie and Annie were next door. No one seemed to question whether these sleeping arrangements made sense for two boys (ages 11 and 10), or whether I was prepared to step foot on a cruise ship again. In retrospect, I believe that Olga wanted Poor Eddie to travel so he would be distracted from the custody case, and I was sent along so Eddie would have a playmate. The good news was that I steeled myself to endure another cruise experience, relying on my newly developed interest in ships that flowed from my World Book obsession. The bad news was that the trip was beyond strange.

Eddie and I were the only children on the boat. We wandered the decks aimlessly, played bingo with the senior citizens, and learned card tricks from the ship's social director. We were the only swimmers in the pool. In the afternoon, we took over the stage in the nightclub and crooned into the microphone. We ate our meals nestled in a banquette with Olga, Sadie, and Annie; I had nothing to say to them. Without my mother there to guide them, the three sisters struggled with their decisions about what to order. The meals lasted an eternity. When we were in our small stateroom, I worked hard to keep my nose in a book, limiting as much as possible the risk that I might catch a glimpse of Olga dressing or undressing.

One evening, Eddie and I were sitting in the nightclub listening to a singer perform. Between songs, a ship employee whispered in the singer's ear. She then said into the microphone "Is there an Eddie Bauman here? Your grandmother wants you to return to your stateroom." Eddie was mortified. Of course, Olga's query did not mention me.

There were more island tours—the old fort in San Juan, the synagogue in St. Thomas, a French beach resort in Guadaloupe, lunch at a mountaintop restaurant in Trinidad, and, of course, more shopping and hondling in the duty-free shops of Curacao and the straw-market in Nassau. One of her cousins had told Olga about a "classy" aperitif called Cherry Heering. Taking full advantage of the duty-free limits, we came home with fifteen bottles of it. Those bottles sat in a locked closet in our house for the next thirty years.

'59 Freneau Avenue never seemed as welcoming as the day we pulled into the driveway when we returned from that cruise. But within a matter of days of our return, my parents, Olga, Howie, Sandi, Eddie and I flew to Jamaica for my parents' annual vacation. Other than my parents, it was the first time that any of us had flown. Our flight from JFK was delayed for hours, and the longer we waited the more agitated Olga became. Every fifteen minutes or so, she returned to the flight insurance kiosk to increase her air crash coverage. If anything had happened to our flight, Sadie and Annie would have been extremely wealthy.

The old plane that finally pulled up to our gate looked as if it was held together by spit and duct tape. Olga could barely summon the nerve to walk down the jet way. We arrived in Jamaica after dark, and still had a two-hour ride to our hotel on a pothole-laden road. We arrived late at night at the small resort that my mother had identified through some brochure. Our rooms were in bungalows with jalousie windows that were always open. As we settled in after our long day, Olga and my parents saw some small gecko lizards on the bedroom walls. My father immediately called the front desk and demanded that something be done about it. Two Jamaican boys, no older than Eddie and I, arrived at our room and chased the lizards with brooms. Olga announced that she was not staying in this dump. I had an asthma attack and sat up in a chair all night.

Early the next morning, my parents left to look for another hotel. We moved that day to the newly-opened Playboy Club up the road. In contrast to the low-key hotel we left behind, everything about the Playboy Club was on a grand scale. Our rooms were located in a modern high-rise white concrete building with sunken living rooms and flower-laden balconies that overlooked the sea. A large bar sat at one end of the pool complex, from which Playboy Bunny waitresses in bikinis adorned with

110

cottontails served tropical cocktails to the darkly bronzed guests lazing on lounge chairs in the Caribbean sun. Beyond the pool, a large tower contained an elevator leading down to the beach, ensuring that no one would have to use stairs during their vacation.

The lobby and public rooms, with their upholstered sofas and dim lighting, were decorated to look like Hugh Hefner's bachelor pad. Framed centerfolds hung on the dining room wall, and nubile waitresses in fishnet stockings, high heels, and the traditional cinched satin Playboy Bunny costumes patrolled the room. For an eleven-year-old boy, it was a dream come true.

As with most of our family vacations, we were on the Modified American Plan—breakfast and dinner at the hotel were included, but lunch was extra. My parents and Olga gorged themselves at breakfast so they could skip the lunch for which they would have had to pay. But Olga could not last all day without eating. At breakfast each morning, she wrapped rolls and muffins in napkins and shoved them in her purse, a "little snack" for later in the afternoon.

We took one excursion away from our hotel, a river tour on long bamboo rafts propelled by young men with long poles, the Jamaican equivalents of Venetian gondoliers. How Olga managed to climb aboard the tipsy craft in her dress and orthopedic shoes remains a mystery. It rained for most of the balance of our stay in Jamaica, so Eddie and I spent our time shooting pool with dirty old men in the hotel lounge, while Bunnies brought us drinks. Maybe this was the education my parents envisioned for me in place of all the school I was missing. I certainly was not keeping up with whatever was happening back in Mr. Bragdon's class; the only assignment he gave me for the four weeks of school I missed was to keep a journal of my travels. I hope he enjoyed my descriptions of the Playboy Bunnies.

When I finally returned to class, we began studying the Middle Ages and Gothic architecture. Mr. Bragdon was now off his crutches, and he arranged a class trip to New York City and the Cathedral of St. John the Divine, the Gothic design of which mirrored some of the great cathedrals of Europe. When we completed our tour of the church, we still had some time before we needed to get on the bus for our return to

Matawan. Mr. Bragdon decided to take us on a quick walk to the nearby campus of Columbia University. As we entered the campus gates at 116th Street and Amsterdam Avenue, I was amazed. I knew nothing about Columbia at that time, and did not expect to find a bucolic college campus with ivy-covered buildings and grass covered quadrangles in the middle of Manhattan. I had never seen anything like it.

After the school year ended, we returned to Northwood for our second summer at camp. On July 1, the same day we left on the train to Utica, the judge rendered his decision in the custody case, ruling against Irving and granting custody to Olga. The judge had this to say about Olga and my parents:

"The grandmother, Mrs. Sloan, is a very high type individual, being intelligent, successful in her business, and having a very strong family tie with all members of her family, perhaps reminding her of the old world from which she came.

"The daughter Helen and her husband fall exactly into the same category as being high type individuals, the daughter having a college background, having had a position that she has had for some time, and the husband appearing well demeaned and a successful salesman in the business owned and operated by Mrs. Sloan."

But the heart of the judge's opinion focused on Irving's behavior:

"He began to spend more and more time away from his home, business wise and socially, and it can be concluded from the facts that this father gave less and less attention to his children and he gave very little attention to his children. He stopped eating dinner with them, he isolated himself in his apartment when he was home, and made it rather difficult for his children when they desired to have his company. He made no efforts to be in the company of or to otherwise foster and develop and let blossom the natural love and affection that a parent would have for a child.

"He was so busily engaged in his business, yet when he took his vacation they were alone, and at no time during all these years did he find time to spend an entire day with them, kindling and building in the hearts and minds of these young children the love and affection that should be there; and as this developed, running parallel with it, almost as a necessity,

112

as two and two equals four, and as his contacts grew less and as the relationship between him and his children grew more foreign, so did the relationship between these children and their grandmother grow closer."

My mother called us shortly after we arrived at camp to tell us the news. Olga had prevailed, Bob Friedlander became her hero, and life at 59 Freneau Avenue returned to what passed for normal in our family. Sandi and Eddie were relieved. So was I. Despite all the time I spent daydreaming about a different way of life, I did not want to split up the four goonks.

Although Irving lost custody, he was awarded visitation rights. Sandi and Eddie had to go to the small apartment that he and Pearl had moved to in Matawan once a week. They dreaded those visits. Pearl badmouthed Olga, and Irving cross-examined his children about what Olga was saying about him and what was going on at our house. He talked about how someday he would write a book telling his side of the story. Irving constantly showed Sandi and Eddie photos or home movies of Charlotte, but he never let them have any of them, nor did he let them have any of Charlotte's belongings. When Sandi and Eddie returned, Olga questioned them incessantly about what Irving and Pearl had said. After a while the visits became more sporadic, until they just about stopped altogether, especially after Irving and Pearl adopted a baby boy and moved to another town.

Chapter Twenty-Three

My father had a family, too. It was just that sometimes it did not feel that way, since we were so immersed in our life among my mother's relatives.

My paternal grandparents Harry and Lena Selinger lived in a small apartment in Highland Park, just across the Raritan River from New Brunswick (where my father was born and raised) and 25 minutes from Matawan. They were a quiet and serious couple who had little to say to their grandchildren. They rarely smiled. My parents, Howie, and I went to visit them about once a month, crowding into their tiny living room on a Sunday afternoon for what seemed like an interminable number of hours. While the adults engaged in a minimal amount of conversation while they drank coffee and ate babka, Howie and I passed the time watching sports on the small television set, kneeling on the floor by the coffee table where Lena had placed a small bowl of potato chips and a glass of Coke for each of us. I devised a game of dunking one chip at a time into my soda, the goal of which was to fill any air bubbles in the chip with liquid and then get it into my mouth without spilling a drop. The longer I could make the game last the better.

As a reward for enduring these visits, my parents almost always stopped at McDonald's on our drive back to Matawan. The first branch of the chain to open in central Jersey was right on the route between Highland Park and Matawan, and my mother became an immediate devotee. As much as Howie and I enjoyed our burgers and fries, I think these forays into the world of fast food were more for my mother's benefit. While she rarely sat and ate meals with us at home, and seemed to subsist on minimal amounts of food, she had a weakness for fast food when she was away from the house. She often drove with a burger and fries in her lap.

Olga was condescending to, and dismissive of, Harry and Lena. In her view, they had "nothing," and Lena was not worthy of Olga's attention or conversation since she was not a businesswoman. Olga made sure to tell Howie and me repeatedly that my father's family did not compare to the Sloan's and the Ungar's. My father was clearly upset when he overheard these conversations, but he never said anything.

Each summer on the evening before we left for camp, my father made Howie and me call Harry and Lena on the phone to say goodbye. Those calls were torture, as neither my grandparents nor I had anything in particular to say to each other.

My father was the second oldest of four Selinger children, all of whom were extremely tall which seemed incongruous as Harry and Lena were relatively short. My Aunt Ellie was quiet and reserved, the opposite of her loud and opinionated physician husband, Manny Katz. Manny and Ellie and their two children, Judy and Jeff (who were the same ages as Howie and me), lived in New Brunswick in the same house where Manny's practice was located. We rarely saw them there, as they usually stopped by Harry and Lena's during our Sunday afternoon visits.

My Uncle Jerry was my father's best friend. A dentist, he was a friendly and gentle soul, thin and athletic. Jerry played football at Rutgers, and unlike my father, he remained active as an adult, an avid tennis player, swimmer, and diver. Jerry lived in East Brunswick in a quintessential 1950's split level with his wife Pearl and their daughter Janice, who was a few years younger than me. His dental office was in the small town of Spotswood, Pearl's hometown, and whenever my father was in the area making sales calls for Sloan Products, he would stop by to see Jerry. Jerry was a Rutgers sports fan, and my father, Howie, and I joined him at many Rutgers football games in New Brunswick.

As a child, I envied my cousin Janice and her life in a small nuclear family with their single-family house in a suburban sub-division and a Ford Thunderbird in the driveway. I failed to notice that Pearl was bossy and demanding, placing strict limits on Jerry and how he spent his time. Pearl did not like to socialize with Jerry's family, so we usually saw my uncle either at our dental appointments (he treated Howie and me) or at Rutgers games.

My Aunt Ceil was my father's youngest sibling. She was a school teacher. We attended her modest wedding to a man named Harold Cohen when I was about six. My main memory of that event is watching my cousin Janice performing her role as flower girl, dropping petals as she walked down the aisle. Harold and his brother owned an industrial cleaning service in Queens. After they got married, Ceil and Harold moved to an apartment in Flushing, and eventually to a house in Roslyn on Long Island, where my aunt taught second grade. Harold's brother Izzy bought a house on the same block.

Ceil and Harold had two children, my cousins Mark and Beth, who were ten and thirteen years younger than me. Their family always seemed to be in a state of crisis. We heard constantly that Harold's business was on the verge of bankruptcy, and whenever we were with him we were subjected to his racist diatribes about the "lazy and shiftless shvartzas" who worked for him. As Harold's business declined, he and Izzy had a falling out and stopped speaking to each other, even though they lived only three houses apart. For reasons that I never understood and were never explained, Ceil and Jerry's wife Pearl also did not speak to each other, so Jerry always had to visit his younger sister without his wife. Sometimes it was hard to keep track of who was not speaking to whom.

My father also had a number of cousins, whom we only saw every year or two—Bernie, the Ford salesman, his brother Jules, an effete professor at NYU (although no one seemed to know what subject he taught), and a couple named Lois and Lenny. To this day, I do not know whether it was Lois or Lenny who was related to my father. Lena's maiden name was Rose, and she also had a sister named Rose. Yes, Rose Rose. Rose had two daughters who were both over six feet tall. One of them, my father's cousin Helen, was married to a man named Ted Silver. Theirs was a family of giants. Ted was about 6'5", their daughter Babette was 6', and their son Lewis, who was the same age as me, was 6'9". I barely made it to 5'11", and could not understand why there was not another inch or two to spare for me from these titans to whom I was related. Lena also had a brother named Nat, who owned the haberdashery store in which my father worked while he was going to college. With the demands that Sloan Products and Olga placed upon my parents, and particularly my mother, our contact with this part of my father's family was limited.

We had much more interaction with Olga's extended family. Olga had a first cousin whom we saw on a regular basis, her cousin Ida. Ida was as sweet as can be, and was always solicitous of Olga's grandchildren. She lived in the Bronx with her husband Morris, a customs inspector, and their sons Mark and Joseph. Mark was ten years older than me, Joseph seven. One summer when he was in college, Mark had a job at a company about thirty minutes from our house. He was staying with relatives of his father, but every night after dinner he showed up at 59 Freneau Avenue and worked with my family packing orders at Sloan Products. That was his social life for the summer.

Olga's other first cousins were the children of her Aunt Rose Lubin, my great-grandfather Victor Ungar's sister. Olga had repaired her relationship with her aunt, notwithstanding that Victor did not speak to his sister for decades after Rose absconded with his hat patterns shortly after the turn of the century. Rose was still alive when I was a young child, and our family would sometimes have dinner at her swanky Sutton Place townhouse in Manhattan. Rose had three children, Olga's first cousins Hymie, Clara, and Dottie.

Hymie never married. He lived with his mother Rose and as she got older he ran the family silk flower business. Hymie used to drive to Matawan every few months to visit his cousins. He always arrived in a shiny Buick Riviera—he bought a new one every other year—and on each visit he brought a cake from the Sutton Place Bakery. No matter what time of year or what the weather was, Hymie always wore a three-piece suit during these trips. He sat at the table in the large kitchen with Olga, Sadie, and Annie, drinking tea, eating cake, and talking about business for hours. Sadie and Annie seemed to relish these visits, perhaps because they could relate to their unmarried cousin whose life revolved around a family business.

Hymie's sister Dottie also worked in the family's silk flower business. She and her husband Milton lived in New Rochelle, and we would occasionally visit them there (I remember sitting in their den and watching the winter Olympics in 1964 when I was ten). Milton was a prim and proper man, always conservatively dressed in jacket and tie with a neatly folded handkerchief protruding from his jacket pocket. He had little patience for Olga's grandchildren. Milton worked in advertising, but when Hymie died, Milton started working in the family business with his wife.

Hymie's death led to a falling out between Dottie and her sister Clara. Hymie owned the townhouse on Sutton Place and a country home in upstate New York. There was a contest between Dottie and Clara over Hymie's estate, with both pieces of property ultimately going to Dottie's children. After that, Dottie and Clara stopped speaking to each other.

I began to notice a pattern among the relatives on both sides of my family. They held grudges, and believed that cutting off relationships and communication was an acceptable way to deal with disputes and hurt feelings. They were not exactly helpful role models for a young boy who had trouble expressing himself to his family.

Chapter Twenty-Four

When I was eleven, Matawan changed radically. A new housing development called Strathmore opened, a huge community of two thousand homes built on former apple orchards by the family that built Levittown on Long Island. By the time I started 7th grade, the town's population had quadrupled, including an influx of new Jewish families from the city. Most of Strathmore's male residents commuted to work in Manhattan, changing the nature of our town from a local, blue-collar environment to a white-collar bedroom community. Strathmore even had its own pool club. Valley Drive lost its traditional name; it was now simply known as Route 34, and the orchards that once lined the road were replaced by Levitt homes, strip malls, and fast-food franchises. Within a few years, Matawan had two temples of its own, as well as a Jewish deli. For the first time, the schools closed for the Jewish High Holidays. But we remained loyal to Beth Mordecai, and a part of me still felt a greater kinship with the parochial small town kids with whom I grew up rather than with the throngs of interlopers from Brooklyn and Queens who now populated my school.

Seventh grade was also a transitional year for me. I moved on from the Broad Street Elementary School to the new Matawan Regional High School building. A new middle school was under construction, but not yet completed, so the 7th and 8th graders were squeezed into the high school. In order to handle the strain on space, the middle schoolers were put on a split schedule: in 7th grade, I went to school from 7:00 a.m. to 11:30, with no gym and no break for lunch; 8th grade was the same, except our hours were from noon to 4:30. The overpopulation of the building also meant that the middle school children had no lockers. We had to carry all our books and our coats from class to class, and then bring the whole pile home every night. Eddie and I hardly saw each other these two years, as our schedules were completely different.

For the first time, the students were "tracked" by academic ability, so all my classes were with the best students, including a large number of kids newly arrived in Matawan from the city. As usual, my grades were excellent, but the main focus of my parents that year was Howie, who was a junior in high school. He was first in his class, well on his way to becoming valedictorian, and my year in 7th grade was filled with family trips to visit the Ivy League campuses that Howie hoped to attend. I accompanied my parents and Howie on each of these tours: Harvard and Yale, Penn and Princeton, Cornell and Dartmouth, and Columbia (somehow Brown escaped my brother's interest).

Just as my parents were focused on my brother and his looming college choices, Olga was fixated that year on Sandi and Eddie. The custody decision had only recently come down in her favor, and more than ever she needed to know where Sandi and Eddie were at all times. In addition, Olga was monitoring closely Sandi and Eddie's visits with their father that the court had ordered.

It was in this context that my 7th grade schedule provided me with more freedom than I had ever experienced. Most days after school, my classmate Dan Craparo (a longtime Matawan resident like me) and I went immediately to his house across from the high school where his mother served us pasta and meatballs for lunch. We then played basketball until the middle of the afternoon on the court that Dan's mason father had built. This still gave me enough time to walk home, do my Sloan Products' chores, and complete my homework.

I also started going into the city by myself. Many Saturdays, I took the bus to the Port Authority terminal, where my Camp Northwood buddy Arnie Engelman met me. We either spent the afternoon playing pinball and skeeball in the grungy arcades of Times Square, or took the subway to Arnie's Greenwich Village neighborhood where we hung out in Washington Square Park and then wandered in and out of record stores until it was time for me to catch my bus back to New Jersey.

Seventh grade was also a time for another type of development for me. Howie, who was fifteen, and I were showing our first real interest in girls. My mother must have picked up on this and got us a subscription to Playboy, because in our household whenever one of the goonks expressed an interest in something it was immediately encouraged (although this was a little different than music or art lessons). Each month when the latest edition arrived in its brown paper wrapper, I could not get to my room fast enough to explore its contents. Howie and I maintained our burgeoning magazine collection under our bed. I soon began flipping through the pages of our special library on a daily basis, just as I had with the World Book a few years prior. I started to believe that there was a world of perfectly shaped, blemish-free women waiting for me beyond my small-town world.

My reading interests in junior high were not limited to the stack of magazines under my bed. I had moved on from comic books and the "Tom Swift," "Hardy Boys," and "Chip Hilton" series and was now tackling serious literature. We read "Silas Marner" and "Great Expectations" in school, along with the typical assortment of short stories by Poe and O. Henry. Soon I was making my first forays into Hemingway and Steinbeck, with some Melville and Hawthorne thrown in for good measure. My compressed schedule at school left me plenty of time for reading on my own.

My time, however, was far from my own. My bar mitzvah was scheduled for October, 1966, at the beginning of my 8th grade school year. That meant that my preparatory studies at Beth Mordecai ratcheted up during 7th grade. By the spring of that year, my Saturday and Sunday morning obligations were expanded to include one evening a week meeting with Cantor Edelstein to learn the chants of my Torah and Haftorah portions.

The other major event in 7th grade was my introduction to my new classmate, Bruce Conrad. Bruce and his family had moved from the city to Marc Woods, another new subdivision in Matawan. Bruce was short and pudgy, with a mane of curly blond hair. Bruce's most notable feature, however, was his wise-ass personality. He was full of biting humor and sarcasm, and had the ability to bust me up in the blink of an eye. Bruce spent the next five years trying to get me to follow him down a misbegotten path of wildness. Sometimes he was successful.

When the school year ended, we returned for another blissful summer at Northwood, where I was re-united with Engelman and

Saltman. At the end of the summer season, after we had returned from camp, seven of us (Olga, my parents, and the four goonks) were scheduled to spend Labor Day weekend at the beach in Wildwood Crest, New Jersey to celebrate the end of Sloan Products' busiest time of year. The night before our trip to Wildwood, Olga fell down the stairs to the basement of our house during one of her 3:00 a.m. strolls. She broke her nose, bruised her ribs, and got two black eyes. An ambulance and the family doctor came and the whole house was in an uproar. I slept through the whole thing. When I woke up in the morning, most of the family was sitting around the kitchen table looking exhausted. "When are we leaving?" I asked. Everyone looked at me like I was the village idiot.

Eighth grade began. Unlike 7th grade, the odd hours of our split schedule left me little free time. I spent my mornings doing homework or working in the office before leaving at 11:45 to go to school. I rarely got home before 5:00, and at the beginning of the school year the final tune-ups for my bar mitzvah ate up whatever time I had.

My grandfather Harry Selinger announced that he wanted to buy me a tallis for my bar mitzvah. My father dropped me off at my grandparents' apartment in Highland Park, where Harry was waiting for me. It was the only time we were ever alone together. We got in his old sedan and I proceeded to hold my breath as he drove. He barely stopped at intersections as he muttered about the other drivers on the road, and whenever we hit a bump I bounced high enough to hit my head on the ceiling of the car. As was usually the case when I was with him, we had little to say to each other. We ended up at a store that sold Jewish religious articles, where Harry spoke to the owner in Yiddish. The proprietor showed us a few tallit, which Harry rejected with a brush of his hand as he said "feh." Finally, we were shown one that met with Harry's approval, and the transaction was completed. On the way back to his apartment, Harry and I stopped at a produce market. He stood in front of the display of grapes, sampling a few from several bunches. He bit into each one, and then exclaimed "Sour" as he spit the grape on the floor. We left without buying any grapes. I was in no hurry to spend any more time alone with my grandfather.

As October approached, my big event became a focus in the house, but certainly not the only one. My brother was working on his college applications, and Sandi who was now a high school junior, was starting to look at schools. But for one weekend, at least, I had my family's attention. The Friday of my big weekend, my parents let me skip school. That day, my mother and I drove together to the Lower East Side to pick up platters of smoked fish for the Kiddush following the Saturday service from Russ & Daughters, the famous smoked fish emporium on Houston Street. It may have been the only time that I spent a day alone with my mother. I decided to ask some questions:

"Is this the neighborhood where the Ungars lived?"

"No, they were a little further uptown on Second Avenue. But they shopped down here sometimes."

"Where did they go to school?"

"I don't know exactly, somewhere near where they lived. Did I ever tell you about when Grandma switched schools?"

"I don't think so."

"Well, when she was about your age, she decided that she did not like the school she was going to. So one day she went to the office of a school she thought would be better and somehow talked her way into being transferred. She never told her parents."

"She bluffed them to get what she wanted."

"What do you mean?"

"It's a trick you use in poker, something Grandma taught us." We pulled up in front of Russ & Daughters and then drove back to Matawan amidst the odors of lox, sable, whitefish, and sturgeon.

At the Saturday service of my bar mitzvah, I tried to stand tall to the full extent of my skinny 5'3" frame, proudly showing off my new three-piece blue suit, the tallis that Harry bought me draped around my neck. My mother wore a gray suit with gray fur trim around the collar, the cuffs, and at the bottom of the skirt, with a matching gray fur-trimmed hat. At the Sunday reception, she wore an aquamarine satin dress covered in dangling rhinestones. When we danced the obligatory mother-son fox trot, my head came to the middle of her bejeweled chest. My father watched proudly, smoking a cigar that seemed about a foot long, a glass of Chivas in his hand.

The highlight of the weekend for me was the arrival at the reception of my Camp Northwood girlfriend, all the way from Long Island. When she saw me greeting guests at the entrance to the catering hall, she ran up to me, threw her arms around my neck, and kissed me. The years of preparation for my bar mitzvah all became worth it as I watched the jealous stares of Dan Craparo and my other Matawan schoolmates. I think her name was Barbara, but I really do not remember.

As with any Sloan event, the food took center stage. The menu at the Chanticler best sums up the excessive nature of the event. I still have the menu for my Sunday reception: Hot Hors d'oeuvres: Tart Shells Portuguese; Croquettes Navajo; Cantonese Egg Rolls with Sauce Anglaise; Mushroom Crowns Graham; Petite Potato Fritters MacIntosh; Onion Gateau; Chicken Livers Monticello; Meatballs Lindstrom; and Danish Liver Pastries. This was followed by a smorgasbord: Veal Scallopini a la Tiberius; Stuffed Cabbage Hungarian; Chicken Livers Traviata; Eggs a la Russe; Smoked Whitefish; Sliced Lox with Dill; Sliced Sturgeon; Smoked Baby Carp Garni; Roast Turkey Royale; Boiled Beef Tongue Garni; and Caviar. The food was spread across several tables, each with an elaborate ice-sculpture.

A full dinner came next: Fruit Naturale; Tossed Salad; Vegetable Soup; Roast Prime Rib with Stuffed Derma, Potato Croquettes, and Tomato Farci; and Strawberry Mousse and a Bible shaped cake for dessert. And, of course, an open bar throughout; the cocktail of choice was whiskey sours, served in tall fluted glasses. Each table had silver containers holding cigars and cigarettes; there were matchbooks with my name on the cover, too. The room was full of smoke and the laughter of inebriated adults. The music for the affair was supplied by Marty Ames and his Men. While I knew many of the guests—our relatives and my parents' friends—there were also several tables full of Sloan Products' vendors and customers whom I had never met.

As that weekend came to an end, so did my brief time in the spotlight. I returned to my schoolwork and my cache of books. Bruce and I made a movie for our social studies class, a parody of 1930's screen classics; the highlight was the scene in which a small cardboard house blew away as the theme music for "Gone With The Wind" blared in the background.

There was another trip to Miami that winter, but unlike all of our earlier road trips to Florida, this time we flew. And instead of staying at the Colonial Inn on motel row in North Miami Beach, we upgraded to the Singapore Hotel, a high rise in swanky Bal Harbour. With a mall and a Saks Fifth Avenue across the street, Olga was all set. While we were in Miami, Diana Ross and the Supremes were headlining the show at the nightclub at the Eden Roc, a glitzy hotel in the heart of Miami Beach that was beyond our increased vacation budget. Sandi, Howie, Eddie, and I begged Olga and my parents to take us to the show. They relented, but as we sat down at our table all the color drained from my father's face as he started calculating the cost of the evening with the cover charge, two drink minimum, and over-priced food. While the rest of us ordered with abandon, he asked for the chopped sirloin (a hamburger in 1960's nightclub parlance).

As the school year drew to a close, my brother again took center stage. Even though he did not succeed in his goal to attend Harvard, Yale, or Princeton, he was on his way to Columbia as valedictorian of the Matawan Regional High School class of 1967. He was only sixteen. The arrangements for his prom, his class trip to Washington, and then his graduation consumed Olga and my parents. The article in the Matawan Journal about Howie's achievement was laminated and taped to the counter in the Sloan Products front office.

Howie's graduation ceremony was scheduled for the same time as my 8th grade graduation dance. I chose to go to my event so I could moon over some girl who did not know I existed rather than attend the high school graduation at which my brother was speaking. No one said a word about my choice, nor did anyone suggest that I had to go to Howie's graduation.

My brother's graduation portended great change for me. When I started high school in the fall of 1967, I was going to have my own room. That was change I could believe in.

Part III

Flying Under the Radar

Chapter Twenty-Five

Howie went off to Columbia with great fanfare and fuss, the first Ivy-Leaguer in our family. As for me, I made a decision as I started 9th grade. I was going to try to apply the lessons I learned about myself from four summers at Camp Northwood to my life in Matawan. I joined the high school drama club and took classes with Eddie and my friend Bruce at the New Jersey Academy of Dramatic Art. I won election as vice-president of the freshman class. I made the cross-country team.

With Howie off at college, I luxuriated in the privacy of my room. No more debate about what records to listen to, no more piles of Howie's stuff everywhere. Posters of my rock heroes were soon plastered all over the walls, with the added benefit of covering the flowered mural Joe the painter had created above our beds. I inherited one of the family's old television sets and stayed up to all hours watching and memorizing old movies, graduating from science fiction and adventure flicks to screwball comedy. I could read without interruption. At least I thought I could.

For some reason Howie's departure signaled to Olga and Charlie that I was fair game, someone who could be lobbied successfully for support in their never-ending war. Or at least they concluded that I was an impartial audience, and, unlike my brother, one who would listen silently to their ranting. At night when I was in my room trying to do my homework, they would constantly come in to list the slights that she or he had supposedly suffered at the hands of the other, only to return to interrogate me about what lies the other was spreading. This could go on for hours. I could not take it, and I started to realize that maybe going unnoticed in our household was not such a bad thing after all.

Soon enough, family attention focused again on my brother. Only a few weeks into his first semester, Howie broke his wrist playing touch football. My parents and I rushed to the emergency room at St. Luke's hospital near the Columbia campus. When we got there, Howie was lying on a gurney, his right wrist contorted like an "S" curve. It was a bad break, and since Howie was right-handed it severely limited him. For the next several weeks, my parents were visiting him regularly, delivering food, doing his laundry, and generally helping him get by. Olga fretted.

In a way, Howie's accident enabled me to return to my normal status in the family pecking order. He had a broken wrist, Sandi (now a high school senior) was applying to college, and Eddie was adjusting to life at the newly completed junior high school building. Olga and my parents had plenty to focus on besides me. But at age fourteen, I was not only getting used to it, I was starting to relish it.

The solitary nature of cross-country training felt entirely natural to me. I began to thrive on the zen of running—it made me more comfortable with myself, and helped me realize that I did not need attention or approval from my family in order to thrive. Although a minor early season knee injury inhibited my freshman year training progress, I competed for the entire season, and placed in the top fifteen of the freshman county sectionals at the end of the season in early December. I did not encourage anyone from my family to come to any of my meets, which were always held on weekday afternoons, and they obliged.

School was also becoming more interesting. I was getting my first taste of Shakespeare. I took a classic literature class and read Aeschylus, Sophocles, and Euripides. The biggest impression was made in my social studies class, taught by Mrs. Sen, a Hindi woman who wore a sari to class each day. She opened our eyes to current events, discussing Vietnam, civil rights, and, later in the year, the 1968 presidential primaries.

As the 1967 summer of love ended, my rock album collection swelled. My father complained as my hair started to reach my collar. I watched reports of the war each night on the evening news. I started traveling to Columbia by myself to visit Howie and to go to basketball games with him, but also to take advantage of his roommate's extensive psychedelic rock album collection. I listened intently as Howie and his friends complained about LBJ, the war, and their respective draft numbers, and as they discussed the great books they were reading as part of the school's core curriculum. The Columbia campus that I had first visited on my 6th grade class trip was becoming more and more enticing.

I started to do volunteer work for the Eugene McCarthy campaign with my friend Bruce Conrad, mainly stuffing envelopes in a local office. I did not tell my parents, and no one questioned where I was. I soon figured out that as long as I kept my grades up, my family was content to let me be.

That spring, we were reading "Romeo and Juliet" in Mrs. Cole's English class. Bruce and I decided to make a rock opera version, our second and last film. Bruce played Juliet, and we used the back stairs to our house for the balcony scene. There was plenty of loud music, and several scenes we stole right out of episodes of the Monkees.

Then the world went mad. Martin Luther King and Bobby Kennedy were assassinated. The McCarthy campaign sputtered. And the Columbia campus exploded when a student strike and building takeover was broken up by a police riot. Howie witnessed it all, including watching several of his classmates being beaten. My parents and Olga were worried sick. I became more politicized. I had regular arguments with my father about the war, the first time I argued with any of the adults in our house.

"Dad, how can you listen to that fat jerk lie about what's happening," I said as I gestured towards the television.

"Are you talking about our President?"

"Your President, LBJ. I sure didn't vote for him."

"Show some respect, if not for the man then for the office."

"I hear people saying shit like that all the time. I don't even know what it's supposed to mean."

"Watch your mouth. You know, I fought in a war to protect our freedom, including our right to elect a president."

"I know that, but he lied about this war."

128

We went round and round, but never got anywhere.

Over the course of my freshman year, I spent more time with Sandi, probably due to my brother's absence. She was dating another Matawan Regional senior, a boy named Howie Edelstein. Edelstein was a Coney Island transplant to Matawan and, coincidentally, best friends with my friend Bruce's older brother, Joe Conrad. Edelstein drove a beat up old Studebaker with a hole in the floorboard right below the pedals. He and Joe cruised around town, often giving Bruce and me hair-raising rides, the radio blasting as they hung their heads out the window.

I soon became a third wheel in Sandi and Edelstein's relationship, tagging along with them to movies and concerts. After many of their dates, Sandi would go to bed while Edelstein and I stayed up watching the Marx Brothers and eating frozen pizza. Needless to say, Olga did not care for Edelstein. For me, that made him all the more appealing.

Olga questioned Sandi about Edelstein the same way she did whenever she heard about one of our new friends or romantic interests, asking "Where are his (or her) people from?" If they were not Jewish, they were dismissed with a wave of Olga's hand as "goyim." But Olga never believed our Jewish friends' ancestral claims. Regardless of their stated heritage, Olga pronounced that they were "Galiciana," a Yiddish euphemism for the common people believed to come from the Spanish region of Galicia. Of course, she proclaimed that the Edelstein and his family were "Galiciana." In contrast, Olga regularly told people that we were Litvaks, the shrewd and highly respected Jews of Lithuanian descent. Except that her family came from a part of Russia nowhere near Lithuania.

The summer of 1968 was my last at Camp Northwood. I worked as a waiter and a junior counselor assisting the water-ski instructor. For the most part, it was another idyllic summer. As junior staff members, Engelman, Saltman, and I had tremendous freedom. The waiters lived in a cabin called Balsam (all Northwood cabins were named after trees). Most of the wait staff lived in the large ground-level portion of the building with two counselors, but the three of us and one other waiter named Steve Kramer lived unsupervised in the small second-floor of the building. We had our own entrance on the side of the building that led to a steep flight of stairs up to our living quarters. We lived up there like Bohemians. We did not see the need to fill wastebaskets, only to have to empty them and carry our garbage down the stairs. Instead, we tossed our refuse into the stair-well, which we swept out when we could no longer maneuver our way through the trash.

One evening when Kramer emerged from the shower wearing only a towel, the three of us grabbed him and locked him in my oversized trunk. We carried the trunk over to the girls' side of the camp, opened the lid, and ran back to Balsam like screaming Banshees.

When we were not working in the dining room, Saltman, Kramer, and I worked on the water-ski dock (Engelman was an assistant tennis instructor). We helped campers in and out of their life belts, adjusted their skis, and treaded water with them as the motor boat began to pull them up and onto the surface of the water. We alternated riding as a spotter in the boat; it was our job to keep an eye on the water-skiing camper behind us as the counselor drove around the lake. Whenever we had a teen-age girl in a two-piece bathing suit attempting to ski, the counselor would reduce the boat's speed just as the girl's chest got to water level. The goal was to drag her long enough so that the force of the water would pull her bathing suit top off. It was a hugely successful operation, but word got out and soon the girl campers started showing up at the water-ski dock in one-piece suits.

Engelman, Saltman, and I also had surprising freedom to leave the camp property that summer. On a few occasions, Arnie and I got rides to Utica, where we played golf on a local public course. But our favorite excursion was going to Grant's, a bar on the far side of Hinckley Lake that served great hamburgers. It was about a half-hour paddle to Grant's in one of the Northwood canoes, and the three of us went several times that summer. On the way there, we paddled seriously, wanting to make good time to get to those burgers. By the time we got back in the canoe to return to Northwood, we were goofy. Saltman sat in the rear seat, and proceeded to do his best to reduce Engelman and me to laughing blobs incapable of paddling. Of course, this meant Saltman ended up doing all the work. His favorite refrain, sung to the tune of "Row, Row, Row Your Boat," was "stroke, stroke, stroke your penis, gently up and down…"

130

There was a bit of a scandal that summer when the new camp owners found a marijuana stash belonging to some of my fellow waiters. The waiters were all summoned to the rec hall to meet with one of the owners, Steve Baker. He placed a metal band-aid container on the table in front of him, its lid open enough to expose some small brown leaves. It was the first time I ever saw the stuff, but at the moment, I did not know what it was.

"I want anyone who knows anything about this to stay right here. If you know nothing, you can leave."

Saltman gave Engelman and me a look that signaled "let's get out of here now." As we hurried out the door, I asked "What was that all about?"

"That was grass, man," Dan responded.

"Grass?"

"You know, marijuana. Somebody's ass is in a wringer."

The summer ended with one final moment of high drama. Our camp cook that year was a burly man named Vinnie, who snarled at the wait staff all through meal time. He worked in the kitchen with his wife, and they fought like cats and dogs. For me, it was like being home. Vinnie had a gambling problem which was not helped by the fact that there was a small racetrack about a half-hour from Northwood. With about a week left in camp, Vinnie's wife discovered that he had blown their entire summer salary at the track. When we came in that afternoon to set the tables for dinner, she was chasing Vinnie around the dining room with a meat cleaver. That night, they packed up their car and disappeared.

The camp's two dishwashers were promoted to cooks for the duration of the summer, and my friends and fellow waiters Engelman and Saltman and I were made assistant chefs and dishwashers. Our first assignment was to make egg salad for 200 people, a job that was clearly beyond our culinary skills. We could barely suppress our laughter as we peeked into the dining room and saw campers and counselors spitting out pieces of shells all through lunch. For our final Northwood experience, Engelman and I were appointed team captains for Color War. As with everything else we did at camp, we laughed our way through the experience.

I returned home just as the 1968 Democratic convention was about to begin. Howie and I watched the events of that week in horror, screaming at the TV and cursing at Mayor Daley. Whatever respect I had for authority was rapidly fading.

Chapter Twenty-Six

In the fall of 1968, I started my sophomore year at Matawan Regional High School. Sandi was now off to college, too, attending Connecticut College for Women in New London. It was now just Eddie and me, back in the same school building again.

MRHS, as we referred to our school, was an amalgam of stereotypical adolescent cliques. At the top of the pyramid were the jocks, strutting through the corridors like peacocks displaying their plumage. Then there were the vocational students, "vocats" to my friends and me, who were biding their time in school until they could find jobs, their free time spent peeling rubber as they sped in and out of the student parking lot in their souped-up Chevy's, Pontiacs, and Ford Mustangs. There were greasers, too, clad in leather jackets and tight polyester pants, the boys with slicked back pompadours and the girls with lacquered and teased beehives piled high upon their heads. We had preppies, complete with penny loafers and Oxford shirts, and nerds with pocket protectors and book bags. The newest group was the hippies, outfitted in low-slung bell bottoms, Frye boots, and work shirts.

As a sophomore, I was not a member of any of these large groups, although I had started my drift towards the hippies; full entry would come the following year. My main daily goal was to navigate my way around the jocks, greasers, and vocats without incurring bodily injury. I shared a locker with a greaser named John Schweitzer, an assignment made strictly on the basis of alphabetical order. He grunted at me each morning as we arrived at the locker. One morning, our lock was missing. When I asked him if he knew what happened to it, he muttered that he needed it at home, so he took it. His look said "What are you going to do about it?" My facial response said "Nothing."

Life in the boys' locker room was similar. There was a football player named Willie Allison who paraded around naked after our gym class, displaying his enormous male endowment that made him a candidate for porn film stardom. About once a week, he appeared at my gym locker (thankfully after he was dressed), asking if I had a couple of bucks to spare. I was a regular source of income for him that year.

With the impending 1968 presidential election, the school had a mock vote by the students that fall. The results summed up the nature of the MRHS student body: George Wallace beat out Nixon and Humphrey.

By the time I turned fifteen that October, I was beginning to master flying under my parents' and Olga's radar. I had also perfected my ability to get good grades without breaking a sweat, leaving me plenty of time to pursue a curriculum I designed for myself. I discovered John Updike, and began devouring his books. I made copies of Updike stories and left them on my English teacher's desk, where they were promptly ignored. I read "The Centaur," a novel about a father burdened by his failed dreams, and immediately related to it, recognizing aspects of my father's life on each page.

I also discovered Joseph Heller that year. My parents were unaware that I spent a large chunk of 10th grade geometry reading and re-reading "Catch 22," which I managed to hide in my textbook during class. The hardest part was smothering my guffaws or responding when Mrs. Hunsicker asked me if there was something I found amusing about rhomboids.

That fall, I was elected president of the sophomore class. The election of Richard Nixon at about the same time appalled me (as did George Wallace's victory in the student mock vote), and I vowed to use my new position to promote my views of social justice. When my fellow officers suggested we sell candy to raise funds for a class ski trip, I told them that the only fundraising I would approve would be on behalf of inner city kids. I defiantly wore a black "Give A Damn" button to our meetings, and when it became clear that I was losing my cause, I stopped scheduling meetings. That led to the impeachment proceedings, about the only thing that Nixon and I had in common. A motion was made to the Student Council to remove me from office, and, after an emotional debate, I hung on by one vote. We never did go on that ski trip, and I made a small contribution to the New York Urban League out of our

134

school dance ticket proceeds. Of course, my family knew nothing about any of this.

That year was also the New York Jets' championship season. Howie and I were raised as Giants fans, our father's football team of choice (Eddie had no interest in sports), but by 1968 our allegiance had switched to the Jets. We loved Joe Namath. The fact that Broadway Joe's long hair irritated our father was an added bonus. Howie and I got standing room tickets to the AFL championship game at Shea Stadium that December, but I ended up watching Super Bowl III by myself. Howie was back at school, and my parents were working in the office that Sunday afternoon. I sat alone in my parents' living room, watching the game on our black and white Zenith. That was how life was for me—I lived in a big house surrounded by relatives, but I ended up doing many things by myself.

By the time I was fifteen, girls were usually on my mind. I went to school dances and did the other things that young teenagers do to socialize, usually to no avail. Olga ordinarily did not make comments on my social life, but she did manage to advise me with these words of wisdom: "Don't get a case of roaming hands" and "Keep a lock on your zipper." I soon discovered that being in the drama club, with its outsized female to male ratio, was an excellent place to meet girls. That's where I met Jackie Parsick, my first serious girlfriend. We had long phone conversations every night and became inseparable, always sitting together at rehearsals when we were not on stage. In the midst of this angst ridden teenage romance, my mother planned our next big family vacation.

The grand trip my mother arranged that winter was a two-week, three-island tour of Hawaii. Since Howie and Sandi were in college, it was just my parents, Olga, Eddie, and me. I shared a room with my parents, Eddie was stuck rooming with Olga. Somehow, my mother booked us in a tour group of about forty people. It was the five of us and a bunch of farmers from southern Illinois, the men all wearing Caterpillar tractor caps, their wives in flowered house dresses. We were held captive with them in a large bus for hours at a time, while the tour guide led the group in sing-alongs. The group's favorite was "I'm a lobster, I'm a lobster, I'm a lobster through and through. But I'd rather be a lobster than an old crab like you." Eddie and I were mortified. I was fifteen, I had a girlfriend back in Matawan, and the last place I wanted to be was stuck on an island with Olga and my parents, five thousand miles from home. I sent Jackie daily postcards, and I made it abundantly clear to my parents throughout the trip that I was miserable. Of course, I got sick. This time it was a whopper of an asthma attack in Volcano National Park.

Our last stop on that trip was Honolulu, where we had a few days free from our friendly farmer tour mates. We spent one of them meeting the Wong family, the soft-spoken relatives of one of Howie's Columbia classmates. Another entire day was devoted to visiting my Aunt Pearl's sister and her husband, not exactly close relatives. The husband was a professor of entomology at the University of Hawaii, an expert in tropical insects, and perhaps the most boring person I ever met. He drove us around the campus and showed us his lab, including a review of a number of his more prized insect specimens. I wanted to slit my wrists.

Not long after we returned, Jackie and I broke up. We were both in the cast of the high school production of "Bye-Bye Birdie" and tried to avoid each other. I soon found a diversion. One of the other cast members was a black girl named Willette Hill, someone I had known since 1ˢᵗ Grade at the Broad Street Elementary School. We soon started dating, spending our breaks from rehearsals walking to town for pizza, or going to her nearby house to listen to records. On many occasions when we were walking together, cars slowed down long enough for teenage drivers to yell "nigger lover" at me.

I made the mistake of telling my parents about my relationship with Willette. I assumed they would be sympathetic, especially my mother who went through the Matawan school system with Willette's mother (who was the Matawan high school valedictorian the year after my mother). I was wrong. They vividly expressed their displeasure. Olga soon found out and started ranting at my parents: "How can you let him date a shvartza?" As it turned out, Willette's parents were equally unhappy about their daughter dating a white boy. The pressure we felt from both our families and our peers was too much. Soon Willette and I stopped seeing each other.

With Howie and Sandi away at college, Eddie and I spent even more time together. We became obsessed with Risk, the board game of global domination, and spent much of our free time in prolonged mano-y-mano battles. The object of the game was to amass sufficient armies to win skirmishes for control of countries, then continents, and ultimately the world. Something about the game set me free from my usually passive self. I attacked recklessly and with abandon, almost always to the point of exposing my flank. Eddie would patiently bide his time, then pounce as soon as my forces became overextended. I rarely won, but the game exhilarated me.

By the summer of 1969, Camp Northwood had closed, the new owners having defaulted on their payments to the Pertz family. Sloan Products was our summer alternative. The four goonks were together again, working harder than ever in the family business. My brother took on the role of foreman, walking through the warehouse with a clipboard of orders to be filled and giving Eddie and me tasks to be completed. We had to change our shirts several times a day to deal with the sweat and the dirt. Since it was 1969, we now wore bandannas around our heads to keep our growing hair out of our eyes as we worked.

At lunchtime, Eddie and I wolfed down some food, and then retreated to my room to listen to our latest album purchases before we had to return to the office. But even when we were not working, Howie continued to issue orders. One day at lunch he told Sandi to bring him some iced tea. She walked over to him with a pitcher in her hand and proceeded to pour the contents over my brother's head as she said, "Get it yourself next time." It was the only time we ever saw her stand up to my brother, or anyone else for that matter.

At the end of each work day, the four of us went swimming before dinner and the evening workload back in the office. On the weekends, we made deliveries in my father's station wagon (Howie or Sandi driving), and continued on to the beach for afternoons of body surfing. Every Wednesday, each of us received a gray Sloan Products pay envelope full of cash. With all the overtime we were working, our savings accounts started to swell. I bought myself a new Gibson guitar.

Of course, spending the summer at home meant more exposure to Olga and her daily tantrums. Sandi was still dating Howie Edelstein, who was living in Washington D.C., where he was attending American

University. He now had shoulder length hair, which he wore pulled back by a leather headband. One evening he arrived at our back door to pick up Sandi. Olga took one look at him and closed the door in his face.

At the end of the summer, my mother insisted that I had earned a few days off. She treated my Northwood buddy Arnie Engelman and me to two airplane tickets to Akron, Ohio, where we visited our friend Dan Saltman. We hung around, not doing much of anything, and watched the reports of the Woodstock festival on TV. After all those summers in upstate New York, we were in Ohio when upstate New York became the focus of the world's attention.

Chapter Twenty-Seven

Watching Woodstock nation celebrate from afar stirred something inside me. As I started my junior year of high school, on the verge of turning sixteen, I succumbed to my friend Bruce's entreaties to embrace the 60's lifestyle. It was a wild ride, but I had become so adept at flying under the radar no one in my family seemed to notice.

By the fall of 1969, Bruce and I had welcomed a third friend into our exclusive group. His name was Mark Ryan. Mark was from a large Catholic family—he had five brothers and sisters—and by 1969 they had outgrown the Strathmore subdivision split-level that the family had moved into when they came to Matawan from New York. That fall they moved into a large ramshackle house on Freneau Avenue only a few hundred yards down the road from our place, one of the few houses on the stretch of highway leading out of Matawan past Sloan Products. Mark had his own room in the house's converted attic which became our haven that year.

Mark was a guitar player, one of the best I ever heard. Bruce and I sat in Mark's room after school to listen to him practice or to argue the merits of Hendrix versus Clapton, two stories removed from any adult interference or supervision. Within a few months, I became his unofficial roadie, helping his band load and unload their equipment at school dances and the other occasional gigs they managed to find. My hair grew long to match Mark's and Bruce's. I wore a fringed vest and a small set of beads under my shirt.

Bruce and Mark loved coming to my house. They nicknamed it The Ponderosa and started referring to my grandmother as Grandma Ben Cartwright. They rampaged through the immense snack collection my mother always maintained, then wandered around the house laughing hysterically at each item in Olga's extensive tchotchke collection. We swam in the pool in our cut-off jeans. When we were not hanging out at one of our houses, we roamed through town seeking out our other long-haired comrades. One of our favorite destinations was the small house where a girl we knew named Gay babysat after school. I doubt the child's mother would have appreciated the fact that three teenage boys sat with her toddler in the afternoons mesmerized by Sesame Street and the Electric Company. There were a number of other hippie girls I chased after that year. One that I dated for a while was a senior at the high school named Donna Borup. She eventually became a member of the Weather Underground. I believe she is still wanted by the FBI.

That year I finally succumbed to Bruce's long-term lobbying campaign to loosen me up. We started smoking dope on a regular basis Then one afternoon that October, we were holed up in Mark's attic bedroom as Mark was demonstrating to Bruce and me how he had finally mastered Eric Clapton's guitar solo from "Crossroads," note for note. Bruce and I were spread out on the mattresses that covered the floor in Mark's room, when Bruce sprung up like a runner out of a starting block. "Hey, don't you turn sixteen this weekend?"

"Yeah, so what?"

"We should go camping, man, that's what. Isn't there some place in the woods behind your house that we could camp, like back by that brook?"

"Camping is righteous," Mark added. "You know, 'going up the country,' 'mother nature's son,' all that shit. It's like we're always telling you, Neil, you gotta be open to new experiences. What would you say to Jimi if he asked you 'Have you ever been experienced'?"

"I don't know. I'd have to ask my parents." That evening, I sat down to talk to my mother while she was engaged in her nightly routine of posting entries to the Sloan Products' general ledger. "Mom, I was thinking that instead of going out or something for my birthday, I'd like to camp out this weekend down by the brook with Bruce and Mark."

"That sounds like fun, dear. What about food?" It always came down to food in my family.

"I figured we'd cook hot dogs or something."

"Okay. I'll pick some things up for you."

140

And that was it. The weekend came and my mother returned from the supermarket with enough food for at least six—hot dogs and buns, marshmallows, corn on the cob, soda, Twinkies and Ring Dings. I packed what I thought I could manage into one bag, found my sleeping bag, and headed outside to wait for my friends.

Bruce and Mark soon came barreling down our driveway on their bikes, bags hanging off the handlebars. Mark had a guitar slung over his back. They were laughing hysterically. They were stoned.

"Hey, it's the birthday boy. Let's go man." We gathered up our gear and started walking past the Sloan Products' warehouse, down the slope that led into the woods at the back of our property.

Bruce held up his hand, signaling us to stop. "Time for an equipment check. Mark—tent and guitar? Check. Neil—food? Check. And look what I have." Bruce unfolded the top of the large brown paper bag he was carrying. "Three quarts of Bud? Check. Hash and pipe? Check. And to ward off the rain, three tabs of Yellow Sunshine. Check." Bruce and Mark started chanting "Yip, yip, yip" as they ran off into the woods. I lowered my head and followed behind.

Our woods were overgrown with no paths. We bushwacked our way through the undergrowth, the bottoms of our pants legs covered with thistles. Finally, we reached the steep embankment that overlooked bucolic Gravelly Brook. The only sound was the gurgling of the stream passing over its rocky bottom. We scampered down the hill and found a level spot along side the brook where we set up Mark's tent. I put some of my summer camp knowledge to work, making a fire ring out of stones and then gathering wood and kindling. Bruce pulled some matches out of his pocket, and soon we had a blaze. He sat down and held court. "I've got it all figured out. We smoke a little hash, get mellow. Then we each drop a tab, wash it down with some suds, watch the stars come out."

I had smoked my share of dope with Bruce and Mark, but acid scared me. So I sat cross-legged next to my friends by the fire as we passed the hash pipe, not saying a word. The sun was starting to set and I got lost watching the rays of orange light filter through the branches of the trees to the surface of the rippling water. Mark was playing his guitar as Bruce unfolded a piece of wax paper in which he had placed three yellow pills.

"Take one, man." I did as I was told, then took a swig from the bottle of Bud that Bruce handed me. Soon I was seeing multiples of everything. I had entered a kaleidoscopic world with three Bruces and three Marks rolling around in front of three campfires, laughing at me. "Look at Neil, man. He is so fucked up." I turned my head to respond, but forgot what I was going to say as I saw repeated images of my head, as if I was sitting in a hall of mirrors.

At some point, I found myself with a hot dog in my left hand and a sharp stick in my right. I stared at them for what seemed like hours, as I contemplated how to bring the hot dog and stick together. I could not figure it out. Then it started to pour.

We scurried into the tent. Bruce and Mark were still laughing, but I was cold, cold in a way that I had never experienced before. I did not know where I was or what I was doing there, only that I wanted to get warm. I held the two parts of my jacket's zipper in my hands, but as with the hot dog and stick, I could not figure out how to bring them together.

In the morning, I awoke to the three of us untangling our barely awake bodies so we could leave the tent.

Bruce was beaming. "You were so fucked up, man. I told you acid is the greatest."

"I don't know. I guess it was all right." I could have lied, said it was awesome, but I just felt guilty, like I had done something terribly wrong. My head was pounding.

We packed our gear and trudged back up the slope and out of the woods. Bruce and Mark took off on their bikes as I climbed the back stairs to my house, where my mother greeted me.

"How was the camping? Did you get very wet?"

"It was fun, I guess. The tent kept us dry."

"A couple of the people who live on Mill Road called to complain about the noise. I told them it was just my son and his friends."

142

"Mark was playing his guitar. I guess we were laughing and fooling around."

"Well, it's nice that you have friends to share your birthday."

I found out later from Eddie that someone had called the police and that a patrol car had stopped by the house. He had an idea what my friends and I were up to and was having a full-blown panic attack when he saw the police arrive. He was about to hike into the woods to warn us when he overheard my mother explain to the cops that it was just her son and two of his friends camping on our property.

Mark, Bruce, and I were in most of the same classes that year. In social studies, we argued with the jocks about Nixon and the war. In English, we offered what we thought were deep and penetrating insights to the story or poem du jour. In French class, however, we were out of control. We were in our third year with Mrs. Perkins, a teacher who had single-handedly destroyed the French language for a generation of Matawan high school students. We sat in the back of the room and spoke English to each other in exaggerated French accents, laughing hysterically. She soon gave up trying to stop us.

There was a difference between us, however. Mark and Bruce had stopped caring about school. Mark planned to become a musician after graduation, and Bruce was not sure he wanted to go to college. But I knew that maintaining my grades was the key to being left alone by my parents. And unlike Mark and Bruce, the lure of the academic world appealed to me. The taste of Ivy League life that I had gotten hanging out at Columbia with Howie and his friends had whet my intellectual appetite, and I saw college as the key to breaking free from Matawan and the world of Sloan Products. I was still consuming books at great speed, now adding Philip Roth, Kurt Vonnegut, Herman Hesse, Twain, Faulkner, and Hemingway to the Updike books I was devouring, and every evening when Bruce and Mark went off to hang out with the rest of the Matawan hippie crowd, I hightailed it home to do my homework.

By the middle of the year, our class rankings were available. I went to the school office, told the secretary my name, and asked to see my rank. She looked at a long list on her desk, wrote a number on a piece of paper, folded it, and handed it to me. I left the office before looking. I stood in the hall, unfolded the sheet, and saw the number "3." I later found out that the number one and two students were Renee Myers and Debbie Richman, two homeworkaholics who, unlike me, were always pressing for extra credit in their classes. It occurred to me that I had figured out how to game the system without having to kill myself trying. I don't remember anyone at home asking me what my rank was, nor do I remember telling anyone.

Although I still devoted a large part of my nights to my books, music became my passion that year. Eddie and I jammed on our guitars, and started and ended the short-lived Bauman-Weiser-Selinger band; we never did manage to come up with a name. I learned to play the harmonica and occasionally sat in with Mark's band. Most important, though, was the music that Mark, Bruce, and I went to hear each weekend. We started going to Springsteen shows at local colleges and at the Upstage in Asbury Park. We took the bus to the city and went to countless shows at the Fillmore East, including Hendrix, Traffic, Santana, John Mayall, and the Allman Brothers Band. There were shows by Cream, the Lovin' Spoonful, Simon & Garfunkel, Chicago, The Band, Judy Collins, Arlo Guthrie, and Laura Nyro. A group of us drove all the way to Port Chester, New York in a fogged-up VW microbus to see Derek and the Dominoes. Yet, no one at home questioned my comings and goings.

After the trip to Hawaii the previous year, I decided I was done with our family vacations. In the winter of 1970, my mother planned a trip to Aruba, including Sandi (during a college break), Eddie, Olga, and my parents. I convinced my parents to let me stay home with Sadie, Annie, and Charlie. They barely supervised me. I turned the Other Apartment into a practice site for a Mark's garage band, since he lacked a garage. I roamed town with my long haired friends. I went to concerts, cavorted with teen-age girls and generally misbehaved. It was the best vacation ever.

I gave up formal school politics in 11th grade, my experience as 10th grade class president having left a bad taste in my mouth. But I organized peace rallies and student moratoriums. That spring, I did not go to gym class for an entire marking period. I hung out at Burger Chef with Bruce and Mark or bummed rides to Holmdel Park, or just stood around in the student parking lot with my classmate Kenny Weiss discussing how we could implement the latest forms of antiwar protests at our high school. Finally, my gym teacher Mr. McCutcheon, who grew up in Matawan with my mother, called the house one night and said to her: "Helen, I think you should know that your son has bought a one-way ticket to Hippieville." But even then, all that happened was my being told that I had to go to gym class. I did, but when the weather got warmer, Bruce, Mark, and I started hitchhiking back and forth to the beach after school.

All the time I was exploring the counter-culture that year, I maintained my interest in sports. I still ran, but no longer as part of the cross-country team—the time commitment interfered with the lifestyle I was exploring. I also played basketball on a Jewish youth league team for which I was the second highest scorer, but when I got benched for skipping practices to hang out with my friends, I quit. I was still a fan, too. Even though Howie and I were Yankees' supporters, we were at the game at Shea Stadium when the Mets clinched the National League pennant. I was also a big Knicks fan at the time—Walt Frazier was one of my idols—and got totally involved in their 1970 championship run. The seventh and final game of the championship round against the Lakers was blacked out on the New York TV stations, but I discovered that for some reason the TV in Olga's bedroom picked up the Philadelphia station that was carrying the game. I watched it by myself sitting on the edge of her bed, the longest stretch I ever spent in her room, which to me was a scary place.

It was around that same time that my grandfather Harry died. The funeral was at his synagogue in New Brunswick. Howie and I were pallbearers, but when it came time to drive to the cemetery my cousin Judy Katz offered to drive. She said she knew how to get there, so we did not pay much attention when we got separated from the other cars in the funeral procession. We got lost. When we finally arrived, everyone was waiting for us. Howie and I rushed to the back of the hearse and completed our job. Lena's children did not want her to live alone, so soon after Harry's death she moved into my Aunt Ceil's house in Roslyn. Our brief monthly trips to Highland Park were now replaced by traffic-filled drives to Long Island.

In the summer of 1970, I went to Europe for the first time. My English teacher Mrs. Seehaus was leading a group of Matawan high school students to participate in a summer program at the Universite de Cannes on the French Riviera, and Bruce and I signed up. I would not let my parents pay, insisting that I was able to foot the bill from my Sloan Products' earnings. My parents made a big deal about my departure, hosting a large family pool party a few days before I left. My Uncle Jerry gave me a newspaper with a fake headline: "Selinger Arrives in Paris."

Our tour started with three days in London. Bruce, some of the other teens, and I went to see the film "Woodstock" in one of the large movie theaters near Piccadilly Circus. Next were a few days in Paris. One night, a group of us went to hang out at the fountains at the Trocadero; we played Frisbee and did cart wheels on the lawn beneath the base of the Eiffel Tower. And then we walked along the Seine. Someone asked "I wonder if the water is cold?" "Let's find out," I responded. I walked to the top of one of the cobblestone ramps that inclined down to the river and turned and waved to my friends. I took a step onto the ramp without realizing it was covered with slick algae. My feet flew into the air; I landed on my butt, and began to slide down the ramp at alarming speed. Soon I was up to my waist in the cool, dirty water of the Seine. I managed to crawl back up the ramp where my guffawing group was waiting for me. I squished back to our hotel.

We took the train from Paris to the core of the program--four weeks in Cannes. There were French classes each morning, but we were on our own each afternoon. We spent our free time lounging on the rocks by the harbor with an assortment of longhaired teenagers from the U.S. and several European countries. Given the relaxed French attitude towards drinking, many of the kids in my program got drunk each night, but none more than Bruce. He quickly became a bore to me, as did the other drinkers, and I moved on. I started hanging out with other kids in my program, students from Copenhagen, London, Los Angeles and New York. I still had a year left in high school, but I was already imagining my life after Matawan and the possibilities that exposure to a less narrow group of friends offered.

While in Cannes, we took a weekend excursion to Geneva. Some of us decided that the towels at our hotel were far superior to the ones

146

issued to us at our dorm in Cannes, so we packed some in our bags. As we were sitting in our bus waiting to depart, the hotel manager came running out of the hotel and stormed onto the bus. "I have just taken a count and we are missing eighteen towels. This bus is not leaving until I get them all back." The other miscreants and I retrieved the towels, handed them to the manager, and slunk back to our seats.

I had one other misadventure after we returned to Cannes. We were not allowed to have overnight visitors in our dorm, but while I was staying there a Camp Northwood friend of Sandi's stopped by to see me. He and his college roommate were backpacking around Europe. Sandi had mentioned where I was, and they figured they could find a free place to sleep in my dorm. I knew it was prohibited, so I had them sneak around to the back of the campus, where they tossed their backpacks to me and climbed over the fence. They slept on my floor that night and climbed out early the next morning. That afternoon I was called into the office of Le Directeur. He told me I was subject to expulsion from the program, but Mrs. Seehaus had pleaded my case. I was placed on probation for the balance of the trip.

Even in Europe, I could not completely escape my Matawan life. My trip ended with a few days in Rome. We toured the Vatican, and as I was standing in the Sistine Chapel staring up at Michelangelo's depiction of creation on the ceiling, a young man wearing a Columbia t-shirt came over and tapped me on the shoulder. "Are you Howie Selinger's brother?"

When I returned home in August, I finished the summer working at Sloan Products. I had spent a year running with Bruce and Mark, and while it was fun, they also made me uneasy, like the night of my birthday camping trip. I was ready for a different experience for my last year of high school.

Chapter Twenty-Eight

I got more serious about school at the start of my senior year at Matawan Regional, not because I felt my grades needed improving—they did not—but because I was motivated by my classes. I took a Shakespeare class with Mr Shaw the best teacher I had in my years in Matawan, and I enthusiastically dove into the canon. I took a class called Senior Seminar taught by Miss Panos, one of our social studies teachers, where we debated current events daily. Unfortunately, I had to suffer though another year of French with Mrs. Perkins.

I started to spend more time with some of the other college-bound students who joined my side of the daily arguments in Miss Panos' seminar—Mike Zaretsky and Elliot Groffman. Willette was also a student in that class, and we soon picked up where we had left off in 10th grade. But we had learned our lesson. This time we did not let our parents know we were dating. One of Willette's close friends was a white girl named Mary McKenna, daughter of our school superintendent. Mary was dating Curtis Edwards at the time, the black captain of the football team, but neither of their parents' approved. So we all engaged in a charade: my parents and Mary's parents were told that we were dating each other, while Willette and Curtis did the same with their parents. The four of us would meet, and then split up into our real pairings until it was time to gather again before we went home. This went on for months, and as far as I know none of our parents ever found out. Eddie knew, but he was good at keeping a secret.

Willette was my first love. Despite our obvious differences, we had much in common. We were long-time Matawan residents, our families established in town for decades before the Strathmore development turned Matawan into a suburban bedroom community, and we had known each other since first grade. But we shared something else. Just as my life at Sloan Products distinguished me from my classmates,

Willette's upbringing contrasted with that of most of the other black children in Matawan. Her father was a pathologist and owned a large medical laboratory; her mother, a former valedictorian, was a special education teacher in our school district. They lived in a split-level with a swimming pool in the backyard. We were completely comfortable with each other.

Since Willette's parents both worked, we had access to the finished basement in her house in the afternoon. Her rec room sofa was the site of my first sexual experiences, our brown and pale limbs intertwined. She told me I kissed like a black boy. I told her we needed to get out of Matawan. We indulged in fantasy conversations, imagining places we could live where an interracial couple would not be hassled.

"Where could we go?"

"I was thinking about Oregon," I responded.

"Why Oregon?"

"Gene McCarthy won a presidential primary there in 1968, so it must be pretty liberal. And it's supposed to be beautiful; you know both the mountains and the Pacific."

"So maybe Oregon is the place."

We kept up these conversations for months, as the charade we were playing on our parents continued. But for some reason, by Christmas vacation I decided I could no longer keep it up. I was working on college applications, and I could not find a way to reconcile the college life I wanted and the fantasy life with Willette that I envisioned. I broke up with her with little explanation, just one more thing I gave up on, like so many activities of my childhood. She barely looked at me the rest of the year.

At the beginning of that school year, I was eligible to get my learner's permit, the first step in the process of getting my driver's license. I had to go to the DMV in Eatontown, about twenty minutes from Matawan, to take my written test. My mother took me in a navy blue Buick Skylark, one of the fleet of cars owned by Sloan Products. I passed the test and got my permit, and as we were walking back to the car, my mother handed me the keys and cheerfully said "Drive home." I had been behind the wheel of a car before, since we had our own parking lot and our own gas pump, my father had let me back up our cars and fill them with gas since I was thirteen or fourteen. But I had never driven on the road.

The Eatontown DMV was near an entrance ramp for the Garden State Parkway, a six-lane highway which was the road we had to take to get back to Matawan. My first experience driving was accelerating onto a highway full of cars going sixty to seventy miles an hour. My mother just sat there smiling, not saying a word. I managed to maneuver up the ramp and into the far right-hand lane of traffic.

I was doing okay until it started to rain. I had no idea how to turn on the windshield wipers, never having had to use them when I was backing that Skylark down our driveway. I was looking all over the dashboard trying to find the wiper switch when I realized I had drifted through the traffic all the way across the highway to the far left-hand lane. My mother was still smiling, still not saying a word. I shouted "Weren't you going to tell me that I was changing lanes?" She said "I knew you would figure it out on your own."

That's the way my mother was. She took things in stride, always acting like things would work out no matter what was going on around her, and if she was anxious or nervous or upset, you could never tell by looking at her. During the months that I was learning to drive, she never told me what to do or how to do it; she just sat and smiled and let me fend for myself. Not like my father, who was constantly barking out commands: "Speed up," Slow down," "Accelerate into the curve," "Watch out for that car," "STOP!"

When I turned 17 that fall, I passed my road test and got my driver's license. Other than having to make the periodic Sloan Products' delivery, I had complete freedom. There were no restrictions, no questioning about where I was going or with whom. I would drive around with Mike, Elliott and a carload of other teenagers all night, then stop at the local Hess station and buy a dollar's worth of gas, enough to buy three gallons. We went to more Springsteen concerts at the shore and more Fillmore shows. There were nightly visits to Matawan's drive-thru convenience store, where my friends and I pestered the clerk at the

150

window with our snickering requests for Coke and Twinkies to go. But most of our meanderings were limited to the weekend, unlike the manner in which I spent every afternoon wandering around Matawan with Bruce and Mark the prior year.

My college application process that fall was not the big production it had been for Howie and Sandi. I went on two day-trips with my parents to look at a couple of schools, but mostly I flipped through some catalogues and course listings. I knew I was going to apply to Columbia, and maybe one or two other top schools, and beyond that I did not see the point of spending a lot of time on the whole thing. I eliminated a couple of schools I thought I was interested in because their applications were too long and I could not be bothered. Our school guidance counselor was useless. I spent all of two minutes with him listing the schools to which I intended to apply. He said "Sounds good" and we were done.

I took a serious stab at acting that year. I had the lead in Noel Coward's "Blithe Spirit," the part that Rex Harrison played in the movie, followed by the part of the Tin Woodsman in "The Wizard of Oz," a production that toured all the local elementary schools. We did "The Matchmaker" for our senior play, in which I played Cornelius, the second male lead. I think I handled it all well, but I discovered that I had no particular passion for acting.

Notwithstanding my efforts to segregate myself from the lunacy of life at Sloan Products, the nature of our life jumped up and bit me one Saturday that year. I was sitting at the desk in my room and I could hear Olga yelling all the way from the other end of the house. I shook my head, wondering who was the victim du jour. I was trying to write an essay for Monday's English class about Keats's "Ode on a Grecian Urn," but it was hard to articulate my views on the meaning of truth and beauty while my grandmother was lacing into some poor member of my family. I got up to close my door when I saw my father standing in my room. Even though my parents' bedroom was only a few steps down the hall, he rarely came in here, especially once my brother went off to college. He looked ashen, and despite his 6'2", 250 pound frame, he appeared withered and small.

151

"Son, what are you doing today?"

"Nothing in particular. My homework, maybe hang out with my friends."

"I need you to help me. We have to go to one of my customers and pick up some merchandise."

"Pick up? I don't get it. Don't you mean make a delivery?"

"I'll explain on the way. We need to take the van, so make sure it has gas. And take a hand truck and some empty boxes."

I pulled the small truck to our gas pump, filled the tank, and then backed into one of the loading bays, where I gathered a stack of empty boxes from the large pile just inside the warehouse door. I grabbed a hand truck, threw everything in the back of the van, and waited for my father. He was loping across our parking lot with the slow, measured steps that signaled that he was up against it, that he felt that things were crashing down upon him

My father climbed into the passenger seat of the van and lit a cigar. "We're going to Twin Rivers Variety, son. Go out Old Tennant Road to Route 33. Then it's a straight shot."

I thought I knew all my father's customers, but this was a new one to me. I was pretty sure that Twin Rivers was a big development about thirty minutes from Matawan, but I still didn't understand why we were going there with an empty truck. My father stared ahead, puffing on his cigar. "Go to a good college, Ace. Learn a profession. Be your own man. Don't be like me."

My father occasionally got into these "woe is me" moods after a run in with his mother-in-law Olga, but this seemed different. Usually, I ignored his self-pitying act because it seemed so pathetic. In those rare moments when I thought about what he was saying, when I allowed myself to feel anything, I wanted to grab him by the shoulders and shake him, tell him to fight back or, even better, quit, tell him that I saw a lot of me whenever I looked at him and that it scared the hell out of me. But at this moment, all I was feeling was concern. He looked beaten.

"You know I'm going to college. Anyway, what does that have to do with Twin Rivers Variety?"

"I thought this was the one, Neil. It's a big new store, only a few months old, and no competition to speak of where it's located. I got my foot in the door before they opened and convinced the owner to let us be the exclusive supplier for most of his inventory. I loaded him up, toys, paper goods, school supplies, our whole line. This was the opportunity I've been waiting for, landing the big customer that would finally prove to your grandmother how valuable I am."

I shook my head.

"The owner called me this morning. He's filing for bankruptcy on Monday. He said we could come today and take back anything that came from Sloan Products as a credit against what he owes us. Once he files, everything gets tied up in the courts for years and we might not see a dime."

"How much does he owe?"

"Close to $30,000. I extended him credit on all his purchases."

Credit was a toxic concept with Olga. She paid all her bills on time and expected the same from her customers. Yes, there were exceptions, but only for established customers down the Shore whose business was largely seasonal. A new suburban variety store did not satisfy the criteria. And to make matters worse, he probably had to go to Olga like a dog with its tail between its legs to tell her what happened. She likely already knew to the penny how much Twin Rivers owed, since she monitored the Sloan Products' books like a hawk. I had not paid attention to the details of Olga's Saturday morning rant, but I could now imagine it word for word. I had heard it a hundred times: *Who's crazy here? $30,000 of credit to someone I've never heard of? That's my money you're giving away, my merchandise that I paid for. Do I have to remind you how hard it is to turn $30,000 of profit on our margins? I never should have trusted you.*

"So that's what all the yelling was about today."

He nodded.

"You should tell her to fuck off, Dad."

"Watch your mouth. I can't do that."

"Why not? What could she do that she hasn't done to you already? It's not like she's going to fire you." I pulled into the Twin Rivers parking lot.

"I can't do that to your mother."

"Speaking of which, where was she during all this? Did she stick up for you?"

"Don't refer to your mother as she, it's disrespectful. Your mother is in a difficult position when it comes to your grandmother."

By the time I entered the store, my father was deep in conversation with the owner. I could see that most of the shelves were already empty. My guess was that this guy had already sold off a lot of his stock, pocketing the cash and screwing his creditors, Sloan Products included. I worked my way up and down the aisles, taking whatever was left that looked like something we carried. There were Twin Rivers' price stickers on every item, which meant that we would have to peel them off before we could sell the stuff to other customers, a pain in the ass job. I filled a bunch of boxes, but it wasn't all that much. It would barely make a dent in the $30,000 we were owed.

We rode back in silence. Looking at my father out of the corner of my eye, I could see that he was already bracing himself for Olga's next onslaught. There was no way that he was going to push back. For perhaps the first time, I decided at that moment to follow my father's advice. I was going to be my own man. I was not going to be like him.

After that day, I was ready to move on. I was already thinking of myself as an intellectual, the first step in my vow to not follow in my father's footsteps. I had been accepted at Columbia and felt like I needed to act the part. I read "Ulysses" by James Joyce, which I made sure to carry conspicuously as I walked through the halls of Matawan Regional. I started writing moribund short stories and depressing poetry for Mrs. Seehaus's Creative Writing class. I failed my last semester in her class, but it had nothing to do with the quality of my work.

That spring, Mrs. Seehaus announced that our class would be working on a puppet theater project together with one of the senior art classes—we would write the scripts, the art class would make the puppets,

154

and we would then put on shows for some of the younger kids in the school system. I told Mrs. Seehaus that this was beneath us, that our class was comprised of serious writers who were taking her course to write serious stories or poetry. When she insisted that we all had to complete the puppet assignment, I protested by copying the text of a "Thor" comic book verbatim and handing it in. My parents never said anything about the 60 that appeared on my report card. I probably did not have a chance to become class salutatorian anyway, but that sealed the deal. I held on for third place.

In May 1971, Howie graduated from Columbia. Nine of us (everyone from the household but Charlie), drove into the city for a celebratory dinner at The Sign of the Dove, an expensive Upper East Side restaurant. Sign of the Dove was one of those places that thought being snooty was the equivalent of being elegant. The condescending Maitre 'd grudgingly showed our rowdy group to a large table and proceeded to hand each of us except my father menus that had no prices on them. My father's did, and as the rest of us studied the choices, all the color drained from his face, just as it had years before in the nightclub at the Eden Roc in Miami. One of the items was roast duck for two, "carved tableside." Eight of us ordered the "canard", and a tuxedo clad waiter emerged with a cart with four whole roast ducks. He sliced a few pieces from each, arranged them on eight plates, and served us. As he started to roll the carcass laden cart back to the kitchen, Olga shouted "Where are you going with those?" She insisted that since we were paying for them, we would like them wrapped to take home.

Eddie and I convinced my father that we should order a bottle of wine, something my family never did. A waitress opened our bottle, filled some glasses, and walked away, leaving her corkscrew on the table. Olga picked up the corkscrew and put it in her purse. A few minutes later, the waitress returned to our table.

"Did I leave my corkscrew here? We have to pay for them, and they're expensive."

"No, there's no corkscrew here," Olga said. "You must have left it someplace else."

As the waitress walked away, there was a loud thud as Olga dropped the corkscrew on the floor and kicked it under the table. We finished the meal and filed out of the restaurant, a bag of foil-wrapped duck carcasses in Olga's hand.

Unlike Howie and Sandi, I boycotted my high school prom and the senior trip, as did most of my college-bound classmates. We were too cool for that sort of thing. Graduation came and went in a blink, and soon another summer working with the other goonks at Sloan Products began. We worked as hard, if not harder, than ever. The hours had not changed, nor had the daily battles diminished, but I felt I had almost reached the finish line and was about to put all that behind me. In my free time that summer, I sat by our pool reading "The Iliad," my first assigned text for Literature Humanities, the "great books" course that all Columbia freshmen are required to take. In a few short months, I would be leaving Matawan for New York City and the Ivy League.

Part IV

Just When I Thought I Was Out…

Chapter Twenty-Nine

From the day I arrived on the Columbia campus in the fall of 1971, I believed that I had truly left Matawan and Sloan Products behind. As I stood in line with my parents and my belongings waiting to move into Carman Hall, I met another freshman, Steve Krasner, a skinny kid from Cranston, Rhode Island. Steve knew little about New York and I took him under my wing with a false bravado that was more about bolstering my own confidence than teaching Steve anything. In the weeks that followed, we rode the subways for fifteen cents per ride, went to the Metropolitan Museum of Art, ate Chinese food at the Moon Palace, and drank beer at the West End.

When classes started I embraced with a passion the world of books and ideas that I had entered, and the dreams of a life of teaching or writing that I once shared with Sam on the Sloan Products' loading dock now felt attainable. I limited my visits home. When my parents wanted to see me I encouraged them to come into the city to take me out to dinner. I was trying to convince myself that after just a few weeks, I had been transformed into a New Yorker, no longer a mere teenager from New Jersey. I was letting Columbia shape me.

The idea was to make us into well-rounded young gentlemen. That was one of the theories underlying Columbia's Core Curriculum, the rigid set of required courses that would take up most of our first two years of college. We would be molded into analytical thinkers, able to recognize the difference between Homer and Virgil, or discuss the merits of Locke versus Hobbes. Our eyes would be trained to discern how the Parthenon led to Frank Lloyd Wright, our ears to distinguish Mozart from Bach.

Each of us would be able to speak a foreign language, apply the scientific method in a laboratory, and write a coherent essay. The rigors of the classroom would prepare us for the vicissitudes of life, and we would be able to make erudite small talk at cocktail parties. At least that was the theory. But before any of that could happen, we each had to pass a swim test.

I knew about the test before I arrived on campus. When Howie graduated from Columbia the prior spring, he told me how his closest friend spent the morning of their graduation in the university pool struggling to swim three laps, a task which stood between him and his Summa Cum Laude degree. The test was an odd historical footnote to the development of the Core Curriculum, a quaint notion that the nation's most gifted scholars should also have the ability to swim 150 yards without stopping as proof of the full dimension of their character.

Inside the information packet I received on the first day of freshman orientation was a slip of paper advising me when I had to report to the gym at the end of the week to take the swim test. The pool was located in a subterranean level of University Gymnasium, Columbia's pathetic excuse for a phys ed facility built in 1898. I arrived in the gym on the appointed day along with at least a hundred of my classmates. We were met by a grizzled phys ed professor who instructed us to line up, then to follow him down the maze of stairs that led to the lowest level where the pool was located.

The underground pool area was dark and dingy, redolent with the smell of chlorine and mildew. Suspended over the pool was a rope from which hung colored pennants for each of the eight Ivy League schools. The professor blew his whistle to get our attention, and then barked at his freshmen charges to get undressed, to leave our clothes on the bleachers that lined one wall of the room, and to form six lines at the far end of the pool. Soon we were all pulling off our work boots and loafers, slithering out of our jeans. The sound of belt buckles hitting the wooden bleachers echoed around the room as naked young men began to line up as instructed. No one had much of anything to say.

He blew his whistle again. "The next time I blow my whistle, I want the six of you in the front of the lines to jump in the pool. When I blow it again, the next six jump in and so on. You need to complete three laps. You can use any stroke you want, but no stopping and no hanging on to the side of the pool. If you don't know how to swim, tell me now and we'll sign you up for a swimming class. If you have trouble while you're in the pool, Coach Jones will fish you out." One hundred sets of eyes looked up at the man in the light blue Columbia phys ed department shirt standing by the side of the pool holding a twenty foot long metal pole with a curved hook at the end. "When you finish your laps, report to the young man with the clipboard at the other end of the pool so we can record your satisfaction of the swimming requirement."

The whistle blew and six naked freshmen hit the water. Moments later, six more. Within a matter of minutes, the pool was churning. I was standing near the end of one of the lines, bemused and horrified by the naked mass of future doctors, lawyers, professors, and politicians arrayed in front of me. The classmate behind me was explaining how he had never been out of Texas before arriving on campus for orientation, when he stopped short and said in his drawl "What the hell is that?" I looked down to see a large roach scurrying across the cracked tile floor. The whistle blew. I jumped in the pool and swam off, a well-rounded Ivy League gentleman in the making.

In the middle of the Columbia campus, there is a statue of "Alma Mater," a robed Greek goddess-like figure sitting on a throne. I had been told by one of my brother's classmates that legend had it that each fall, the first incoming freshman to find the small owl hidden within the folds of Alma Mater's gown would become valedictorian of his class. I made it one of my first orders of business on my first day at school. Years later, I learned that I had gotten the legend wrong—the real tale states that a freshman who finds the owl will marry a Barnard student. I met my Barnard student at the end of my first semester.

Her name was Judy Cowan, a freshman from Haverhill, Massachusetts. The first time I saw her, she was sitting on the steps of Low Library, a social gathering point in the middle of the campus. She was wearing a faded denim work shirt with tiny flowers embroidered on the collar and was engaged in an animated conversation with another young woman as she fussed with her thick mane of black, wavy hair. I walked by without saying a word. A few days later, I stopped by a café in the lounge of one of the Barnard dorms. Judy was working behind the counter and as I placed my order we got to talking. I quickly grasped that she was smart and feisty, a spitfire in a 5'1" frame, someone with whom I could debate any academic topic. I asked for her phone number and called her the next day.

Judy did not know her way around the city, so for our first date I took her to a cheap restaurant called Shakespeare's in Greenwich Village, a neighborhood I knew well from my visits with Arnie Engelman and an area where I could show off my familiarity with New York. We talked for hours, and on the subway ride back to campus, she leaned into me and put her head on my shoulder. We made another date. When the time came a few days later for us to meet, I was in the middle of a heated game of Scrabble with my suitemates. Maybe I was oblivious to the time, or maybe it was because I was winning, but I kept Judy waiting for two hours. She should have learned a lesson about my tendency to pre-occupation. I had not changed that much from the chronic daydreamer at the Broad Street Elementary School.

Notwithstanding my thoughtlessness, Judy kept seeing me. We had long dinners during which we discussed books, movies, and our families. By the end of my first semester at Columbia, Judy and I were sleeping together. The thought of spending my long Christmas vacation in Matawan with my family, and without her, was not an inviting prospect. I invited myself to Haverhill, a down-on-its-luck mill town in Northeast Massachusetts. It took three buses and most of a day to get there, and when I finally arrived Judy made it clear that she was not thrilled that I was treading on her turf during her first college break. I spent much of the next few days watching sports with her father and her younger twin brothers.

By the time we returned to school for our second semester things smoothed over. We were in love and inseparable. Judy's friends started referring to me as Mr. Columbia, the college boy that every Barnard student's parents wished her daughter would bring home. My relationship with Judy, and a confluence of other events, shaped the arc of my future plans.

In February of 1972, early in my second semester of college, my father had a massive heart attack. He was driving to see a customer when it happened, and he passed out and crashed into a row of garbage cans along the curb. The paramedics rushed him to the hospital in New Brunswick, where he was in intensive care for weeks. When my mother called me in my dorm room to break the news, I broke down and sobbed uncontrollably. It was as if I knew that this day was coming—I had seen it in the beaten expression on my father's face during our ride to Twin Rivers' Variety a year earlier—and could do nothing to stop it.

I took the first train to New Brunswick, where I ran into my father's sister Ceil in the hospital parking lot. She was crying hysterically. When I made it up to my father's room, I was told by the nurse that I could only see him for a couple of minutes. He was hooked up to all kinds of tubes and monitors. When he saw me, he slowly lifted his arm and whispered "My son, my son." Even though I knew that my father was overweight, smoked, and got little exercise, as I held his hand and looked at him, all I could think was that Olga had done this to him.

On the train ride back to the city, I realized that some of my plans would have to be put on hold. I resolved that I would try and pay for a part of my college costs to ease the burden on my parents. But I also knew that my father's condition meant that Sloan Products might need me. A few weeks later, we started reading Stendahl's "The Red and the Black" in my Lit Hum class. I immediately identified with the tale of young Julien Sorel whose lofty ambitions were constantly thwarted by his background and circumstances over which he had no control. For the first time, I was dominating the discussion in class.

As summer approached, my father was still recuperating and unable to work full time, certainly unable to spend long days driving to see his customers. So when I finished school in May, I volunteered to take over his route, calling on his customers through the busy summer season. Some days he felt up to riding along with me for part of the day, but most of the time I was on my own. While Olga showed uncharacteristic sympathy towards my father at the time, the situation did nothing to diminish her tirades. If anything, her battles with Charlie intensified that summer. I began to understand that spending twelve hours a day calling on customers was an agreeable alternative to being in the office listening to her rants. On as many weekends as I could that summer, I made the 600 mile round-trip drive to Haverhill to see Judy, who was working as an aide in a local nursing home.

As my sophomore year began, I kept my promise to myself and starting paying for my own room and board at school. I got a part-time job cutting sample swatches of material at the Madison Shirt Company in the garment district; I felt at home there, listening to the two brothers who owned the place argue with each other all day long. Between my job, my course load, and typing Judy's papers on my small Olympia typewriter (which she always hand-wrote at the last possible minute), I had little free time, although I managed to play on an intramural basketball team with Krasner and some of our friends. I studied hard, and that spring I declared my major in English, with a minor in Art History. I got all A's in those subjects, but my father started a whispering campaign about my future prospects. At every opportunity, he asked "What can you do with that? How will you make a living?"

Judy and I virtually lived together that year, as she abandoned her roommates each evening to join me in my cramped 10 by 13 single dorm room where we cooked dinners on my small hot plate and spent our evenings plowing through the texts of our demanding course loads. We did not want to spend the summer 300 miles apart, so Judy got a job in Revlon's lab in New Jersey where her Uncle Malcolm was a senior executive. She spent her days charting lipstick colors, returning at night to her Aunt Barbara and Uncle Malcolm's large house in Plainfield, about thirty minutes from Matawan. Sensitive to my father's precarious health, and wanting to earn and save money, I was back at Sloan Products. I spent my days that summer sweating in the warehouse with Eddie, and my nights driving to Plainfield to see Judy. Over the course of the summer, I could see that my father was still not fully recovered and that I would be needed at home for the foreseeable future.

Barbara and Malcolm's house was an expansive old Colonial, filled with large Persian rugs and high quality antiques. The landscaping was perfectly maintained, with mature plantings surrounding a deep-blue free form pool in the backyard. The place reeked of class. One weekend that June, Malcolm and Barbara were away so I stayed in Plainfield with Judy. We went out to dinner and when we returned to the house I went off to use the bathroom at the back of the large entry foyer. I locked the door behind me, a habit engrained in me as a child when I tried unsuccessfully to gain some privacy from Olga's cross-examinations through closed bathroom doors about the state of my intestinal progress. When I was finished, I turned the latch but the door would not budge. I tried and tried without success. I was locked in.

"What are you doing in there?" Judy asked through the door. "You've been in there for twenty minutes."

"The lock is stuck. I can't get the door open."

"What did you lock it for? We're the only ones here. Did you think I was going to barge in on you? Now what are we supposed to do?"

"Maybe you can take the lock apart with a screwdriver?"

"I'm not going to start destroying this house."

It was at that moment that I noticed the small window about six feet above the floor. "I think I can make it out the window to the back porch." I opened it, hoisted myself up, and tumbled to the floor of the porch. Judy was standing above me, her face crimson.

"Now you've done it," she yelled. "I don't understand you sometimes. You better figure out how to open that door before my aunt and uncle get home." She stormed off, barely speaking to me the rest of the evening. Early the next morning, Judy's twenty-one year old cousin David returned. He climbed in the window from the porch to the bathroom and with one turn of the latch opened the door.

Later that month, on June 24, 1973, Sandi and Howie Edelstein got married. They had each graduated college in 1972; Sandi was working for Chemical Bank in New York, and Howie was working in the insurance industry. Sandi's wedding gave Olga another opportunity to take center stage. The wedding was even more elaborate than the bar and bat mitzvah's at the Chanticler. The affair was held at another ornate catering facility, the Crystal Plaza in Livingston, New Jersey. As the family was getting ready to leave Matawan on the day of the wedding, Olga asked me to come into her room and help her get something out of her closet, a shoe box buried deep on the top shelf. I stood on a chair, dug the box out, and handed it to my grandmother. She opened it and I saw that it was full of cash. She took it with her to pay the caterer.

The chapel at the Crystal Plaza had a large *chuppah* with a feathered canopy. The buffet tables were decorated with ice sculptures and intricately carved melons. The film that Olga hired someone to make of the event had a sequence where the melons and other items on the buffet swirled around in a kaleidoscopic effect.

The wedding took place on Olga's birthday. During the ceremony, she had my brother Howie and Eddie walk her down the aisle. She milked the moment for all it was worth, blowing kisses to the guests with broad sweeps of her chiffon covered arms as she slowly made her way to the *chuppah*. Typically, I was relegated to escorting one of Sandi's bridesmaids. The four goonks and our dates (Judy included) were seated together during dinner. For no ostensible reason, I started serenading the bride and groom with "You're Nobody 'Til Somebody Loves You;" Howie and Eddie soon joined in, a three goonk performance.

After they were married, Sandi and Edelstein moved into the Other Apartment at 59 Freneau Avenue, where her parents had lived, while they waited for their new apartment in Fort Lee to be completed.

Chapter Thirty

In the fall of 1973, at the beginning of my junior year of college, Judy and I decided to get engaged. Yes, we were in love, but there was no proposal, no singular romantic moment. I wanted to escape the grasp of Sloan Products; Judy wanted to leave her parochial New England life behind. It never occurred to us that we could accomplish those goals through other means, or that in 1970's New York we could live together with ease after we graduated. For some reason, getting married seemed like the best and only solution.

I went home one Saturday to tell my parents. As was typical with them, there was not a moment during the day when they were both in the same place. I finally caught up with the two of them that evening, sitting on the edge of their bed as they got ready to go out.

"Mom, Dad, I have some news. Judy and I are getting engaged."

"Oh, honey, you're so young," my mother said.

"We're not so young, and besides we're both smart, we do well in school. We'll be fine."

"What will you live on?" my father asked. "What can you do with an English degree?"

"I might go to graduate school, then write and teach. Or maybe become a book editor."

"Those things don't pay much."

"I didn't come here to debate this or ask your permission. I had this harebrained notion that you might actually be happy for me."

"Oh, honey," my mother said, her voice etched with resignation, her eyes puffy and red. I left their room and went back to New York.

The following weekend, Judy and I went to Boston, where we bought an engagement ring at the jewelry store where her older sister worked. Not long afterwards, we went out to Matawan to show it to my parents. When we arrived, my mother was working in the office. We found her at the packing table. When Judy held out her hand to show off her prized possession, my mother said "Best of luck," and continued with her work. Olga walked passed us as if we were not even there.

A few days later, I received a letter from my brother Howie. After Columbia, he began a clinical psychology doctoral program at the University of Connecticut; in the fall of 1973, he was doing his residency at a hospital in Denver, Colorado. He told me in his letter that rushing into marriage at my age was a big mistake and that statistics showed that couples who married young were much more likely to get divorced. He urged me to reconsider. His letter had the opposite effect. I resolved to show my family wrong. I made the mistake of showing the letter to Judy. She felt that my family was conspiring against us, that they were meddling in our lives. She never got past it.

After we were engaged, I took Judy to Greenwich Village to meet my old Camp Northwood buddy Arnie Engelman. The three of us ended up at the apartment of Arnie's parents. His mother's prized possession was the deep-pile white carpet in their living room, which was just beyond the small tile-floored foyer. Shoes had to come off as soon as you entered the place, as the possibility of tracking dirt on the carpet was more than Arnie's mother could bear. On one side of the foyer was a slightly raised pedestal on which sat a number of tall vases filled with flowers.

When it was time to leave, Arnie, his parents, Judy, and I all crowded into the foyer to say good-bye. Mrs. Engelman handed me my long blue overcoat which I twirled around my shoulders with a great flourish, an attempt to demonstrate my Ivy League panache. As I swung my coat, the bottom hit one of the vases on the pedestal, starting a domino effect as they all proceeded to fall over in succession. A trickle of dirty water started to spread across the tile floor. Before any of us could move, it became a torrent, rapidly reaching the white carpet where the brown water leeched into the thick fibers, creating a large dark stain that continued to expand into the living room. As tears streamed down her cheeks, Mrs. Engelman said "Don't worry, it will be all right." I did not dare make eye contact with Judy.

166

As the school year progressed, I focused on my studies and my job as Judy and her parents started to make plans for an August 1974 wedding. I was now working part-time at the Museum of Natural History on the staff of Dr. Margaret Mead, the noted anthropologist, where I was the assistant to her bibliographer, Joan Gordan. I worked on two projects over the course of my two years on Dr. Mead's staff: I organized and catalogued her personal research library, and Ms. Gordan and I read every page of Dr. Mead's collected writings (books, articles, and speeches) and prepared a subject matter index of the work. I was putting my training as an English major and an avid reader to use, and Ms. Gordan let me know at every opportunity that my work was valued and appreciated.

Even with the self-esteem I garnered working for Dr. Mead, my father had succeeded in planting the seeds of doubt about my future in my head. And I still carried with me the memories of our trip to Twin Rivers from a few years before. I was fixated on not following in my father's footsteps, and yet I also yearned for his approval. I was beginning to believe that financial independence was a necessary component of achieving those goals. I was about to get married, and jobs in the liberal arts were hard to come by. I decided to talk about it with Judy.

"I'm thinking that maybe I should do something else after we graduate, give up on the English thing."

"Like what? I thought that's what you wanted to do."

"Yeah, but it's really all about using the language. There must be something else I can do with the English language, and maybe make a decent living at the same time."

"Such as?"

"What about law school? To be a good lawyer you have to communicate effectively."

"I guess, but do you really want to be a lawyer. I've never even heard you talk about it before."

"I don't know. Maybe it's worth a shot. I could at least take the LSATs and see how I do, see if it's an option."

That was the extent of my analysis. I bought an LSAT review book, studied for a couple of hours, took the exam in the spring of 1974 and got a high score. The route out of Matawan that I had mapped out, my carefully orchestrated plan of a life of teaching and writing, was about to take a detour, a left turn down a road more than thirty years long.

In June of 1974, my brother got married in Denver. While he was doing his residence there, he met and fell in love with a Colorado native named Marilyn Strachman; their wedding took place in the temple where Marilyn's family belonged. For Judy and me, the wedding weekend was almost our undoing.

Of course, my entire family went west for the event. For many of us, Judy and myself included, it was our first trip to Colorado. We all stayed in a hotel in downtown Denver. I guess my parents wanted to limit the number of rooms they were paying for, so we ended up with some odd sleeping arrangements. I shared a room with Eddie and my Uncle Charlie. Judy and my Aunt Sadie were roommates for the weekend. I don't know if it was the hotel situation, or a carryover from the letter my brother had sent me when Judy and I got engaged, but Judy was in a foul mood from the moment we landed at Stapleton Airport. She did nothing to hide her feelings.

The day before the wedding, my brother arranged a mountain tour for some of us who had never seen the Rockies. It was cold and overcast as Judy, Eddie, Charlie, and I climbed into my brother's car in front of our hotel. We could barely see the mountains as the highway climbed out of Denver, and as we gained altitude it started to snow. As we made our way further into a high mountain pass, Charlie started asking a series of innocuous sounding questions: "Where do people buy their gas around here?" "Don't they have any restaurants in the mountains?" "There must be someplace for people to shop for groceries?" It was then that we noticed the stench. Charlie finally announced that we needed to find a bathroom, but it was too late. My brother pulled into a small café a few minutes later. Charlie waddled across the parking lot as the rest of us tried to deal with Howie's newly-soiled backseat. When Charlie returned to the car, we drove back to Denver in silence.

At the wedding the next day, Judy was in a snit over some perceived mistreatment by Howie and Marilyn. The tension was palpable. The four of us barely spoke. I was Howie's best man, and I gave a perfunctory toast in performance of my duties. I spent most of the evening sitting at our table with my arms across my chest, wondering how I got into this situation.

The following morning, the Sloan Products' crew (Olga, Sadie, Annie, Charlie, and my parents) were leaving at dawn so they could get back to the office as early as possible. Judy, Eddie, and I were taking a later flight. When we returned to the hotel from the wedding, Judy asked me to come visit her in her room once our older roommates had left for the airport. I heard Charlie leave our room, but I could not find the energy to get out of bed, and I felt uneasy about sneaking past Eddie for an early morning liaison. When I saw Judy later that morning, she was livid. She would not speak to me.

The cold-shoulder treatment continued as we rode to the airport and boarded the flight to Newark. I was sitting between Judy and Eddie on the plane and she proceeded to talk to him as if I was not there.

"Eddie, can you give me a ride to LaGuardia when we get back? I'm going to take the shuttle to Boston. I'm moving back to Massachusetts. I've had it with New York."

"Really?" Eddie replied.

"What the hell are you talking about?" I added.

"So can you do it, Eddie? If not, I guess I can take a cab."

"Are you just going to keep acting like I'm not here?"

At that moment, the plane began to accelerate down the runway as we prepared to take-off. We kept going further and further along the ground without lifting off. I could tell something was wrong, and as I reached over and took Judy's hand, the plane screeched to a halt at the end of the runway. Judy put her head on my shoulder, tears in her eyes.

"This is the captain speaking. We were not getting enough power in the number two engine, so I aborted the take-off. We're going to return to the terminal so the ground crew can check it out."

After a delay of a few hours, we made it back to Newark, Judy returning to the apartment in Manhattan where she was living that summer while she worked in the Columbia library, me to 59 Freneau

Avenue and a summer of work at Sloan Products. We barely spoke about that weekend and got ready for our end of the summer wedding as if nothing had happened.

We got married on August 18, 1974 in Andover, Massachusetts. I was staying in a hotel there along with my family, again rooming with Eddie and Charlie. The night before the wedding, Krasner and a few other college friends took me to a local bar where we played pool and drank beer for a couple of hours. They dropped me off at the hotel, and as I was walking past the bar on the way to my room, my Uncle Manny and Cousin Jeff waved to me to come join them for a drink. Manny kept buying me round after round. By the time I put up my hand and announced that I had enough, the room was spinning. I weaved down the hall to my room, which was now spinning, too. I fell asleep in my clothes and woke up a few hours later with the dry heaves. I spent the morning of my wedding on my knees in front of the toilet, praying that I would feel better if I could only manage to vomit.

Maybe it was my hangover, but I remember little about our wedding. My parents' friends were rowdy, as they usually were at social occasions, but my family's disapproval of my marriage hung over the affair . Judy and I spent our wedding night in the fabulously romantic Howard Johnson's motel in nearby Haverhill. We went to Nassau for a week for our honeymoon where we tried to act like adults, embarrassingly overdressed for every meal. I was not even old enough to gamble in the casino.

Chapter Thirty-One

I started my senior year at Columbia as a newlywed, living in a small, non-descript two-room apartment on the sixth floor of a building on 106th Street and Amsterdam Avenue, eight blocks from the campus. Our two small windows looked out onto an air shaft. The tenants in the building were mostly Hispanic immigrants, with a smattering of Columbia students. Each evening when I returned from classes to our apartment, I walked by four men playing dominoes on a folding table in front of the building, salsa music blasting on their radio.

Being back at Columbia was a safe haven for me. I was enrolled in several small seminars, where my fellow English majors and I sat around conference tables earnestly discussing the implications of literature. I was also still working for Dr. Mead, where I added hours in an attempt to make some more money. Judy had at a job at the Columbia library, and was taking extra classes so she would have enough credits to graduate by the end of the fall semester, thus saving a half-year of tuition. At night, Judy and I spent our time in the same way we had before we were married, cooking the cheapest meals possible (Kraft macaroni and cheese, a complete dinner for only thirty-five cents) and then studying for the rest of the evening in our small living room. The only difference was the nightly battle I fought with the roaches in the kitchen. I also developed a new habit, removing my slightly loose wedding band and spinning it on the table as I read. Judy was constantly after me to have it re-sized.

I still managed to find the time to play basketball and run on the creaky indoor track in the school gym. Krasner and I continued to play intramural basketball together, and our team made it to the league championship game. But Steve abandoned us that night to attend the awards dinner for the school newspaper, for which he was the sports editor. For some reason he had this misguided notion that his goal of a journalism career took priority over his teammates. Left without our point guard, we never had a chance. Judy did not seem particularly interested in my disappointment.

I filled out my law school applications, as I nearly convinced myself that being a lawyer might not be so bad. That spring I was accepted to NYU Law School. Life in New York City would continue. Graduation came, Judy and I both wearing our light blue caps and gowns. There was no big fuss, no extravagant dinner at Sign of the Dove, no over-the-top gift from Olga. Judy and I spent the summer in our hot, airless apartment on 106th Street, from which I commuted to Sloan Products each day. Judy continued working in the Columbia Library. I could not stand the summer heat in the city, tossing and turning each night in sweat soaked sheets. At my urging we spent most weekends in Matawan, either swimming in the pool or going to the beach.

Being in Matawan also meant I was on call for weekend deliveries or other Sloan Products' errands. Judy resented the intrusion into her leisure time, constantly reminding me that she worked hard all week and had no intention of spending her weekend running around for my family's benefit. She rarely offered to pitch in help in the office or with my mother's constant meal preparation responsibilities. I was oblivious to the mutual dislike that was developing between Judy, Olga, and my mother. Apparently, Howie, Sandi, and Eddie were keenly aware of what was happening, but no one ever said a word to me.

Judy and I spent our first anniversary at Island Beach State Park in Seaside Heights, New Jersey with Sandi and Howie Edelstein, some of their friends, and Eddie. A group of us were playing football near the water's edge, and as I dove to catch a pass, my elbow slammed onto the sand, dislodging my too large wedding ring which went soaring into the Atlantic. Maybe it was an omen, or maybe it was just another instance of me disappointing Judy. Regardless, she was livid; she hardly spoke to me on the ride home.

That fall, Judy was starting work as a paralegal at Sullivan & Cromwell, one of the oldest and WASPiest law firms in New York, while I began law school. We started to look for an apartment in Greenwich

Village, near Vanderbilt Hall on Washington Square South, home of NYU Law.

After weeks of searching, Judy and I found an apartment in the Village, in a newly converted loft building on 10th Street and University Place, a five minute walk from the law school. Judy's salary would cover the rent, but we would have little if anything else to live on. We decided I should ask my grandmother for a little help.

Olga had started telling her customers that I was going to law school to round out my business education, better preparing me for the day I took over Sloan Products. Maybe I was her last hope. Sandi was working as an assistant branch manager for Chemical Bank. Howie and Marilyn spent a year in Connecticut while Howie completed his doctorate, but they were about to move back to Denver where Howie would start his career as a clinical psychologist. The day that Howie and Marilyn were scheduled to leave Matawan on the start of their long drive to Denver, Olga threatened to lie down in front of his car. Eddie was about to start his senior year at Tufts (which he attended after he was salutatorian of his high school class), where he was majoring in psychology, also planning a career as a clinical psychologist.

A few days later I was in Matawan for my normal summer work hours. When the office closed for the day, Olga was sitting at one of the tables on the patio, reading the National Enquirer. I sat down next to her. "You shouldn't read that stuff, Grandma. You know that they make it all up, none of it is true."

"Then how can they print it?"

"They just do, they figure people are gullible and that the celebrities they write about won't spend the time and money to sue. Anyway, that's not want I want to talk to you about."

"What then?"

"Judy and I found a nice apartment, only a short walk to where I'll be going to law school in September. She'll be making enough to pay the rent, but we won't have much else to live on. I was wondering if you might be able to help us out. An extra $100 a month would make things a lot easier."

"What about her people?"

"What do you mean?"

"Have you asked her parents?"

"No. They don't have any extra money, and Judy's brothers are both in college right now. I can't ask them."

"That's what you get with Galiciana, nothing. If her parents were willing to do something, maybe I would chip in a little. But I don't see why I should pay everything."

I grabbed Olga's Enquirer in exasperation and slammed it shut. "You know what, forget I asked. I'm sure if Howie or Sandi or Eddie asked, you would say yes in a heartbeat. But never me. I don't need your money." I got up and walked away.

When I got back to our apartment, Judy asked me how it went with Olga.

"Forget Olga. We'll make do without her."

"Did you ask her?"

"Yes, I asked her. She said she'll chip in something if your parents do. I told her I don't need her money."

"That's it? You go back there and demand it. You have it coming to you. Stand up to them for once." She was yelling.

"I'm not going to do that. It's not worth it to me."

"Tell me then, what are we supposed to live on." She was yelling even louder.

"I saved almost everything I made this summer. That will carry us through my first year of law school and then I'll get a job."

Judy stared right through me, turned around, walked into our bedroom, and slammed the door.

Chapter Thirty-Two

Judy and I moved into the apartment at 35 East 10th Street without the financial assistance I sought from Olga. Judy started her job at S&C (as it was called by the firm's employees) and I started my first year at NYU law school. I showed up for my first day of class in a pair of creased khaki's and a crisp Oxford shirt because that is how I thought law students dressed. Most of my classmates were wearing the same jeans, t-shirts, and sandals that they wore in college. It was not the last time that I felt like I did not fit in at law school.

That entire first year is a blur to me now. I made two friends early on—Joel Rudin who had gone to Cornell and Mark Ladner who had attended Yale—and we sat together in all our classes, but there was hardly time to socialize. The work load was oppressive, and I spent what seemed like every waking moment studying. And after my four years at Columbia where most of my classes were small and dialogue was encouraged and nurtured, I found the large lecture hall format and the Socratic method of my law school classes stultifying.

I hardly saw my family that year, and I barely saw Judy more than that. She was assigned to be part of a trial team on a case that lasted for months. She was working ninety to a hundred hours a week, eating dinner at the office, and coming home in the middle of the night. Occasionally, I went down to her office at night and sat on the floor of her small office and studied. It was my first opportunity to view large law firm life, and I quickly concluded it was not for me.

Judy's trial ended that spring, a total win for S&C's client. One of the lawyers working on the case hosted a victory dinner in her Upper West Side apartment. There were eight of us, and the liquor was flowing at an alarming rate. As an attorney-to-be, I felt the need to keep up with the litigators in the room whose glasses were constantly being re-filled. I had three large Scotches before the meal, and then the eight of us polished off seven bottles of wine with dinner. At the evening's end, an ancient bottle of Cognac made its appearance. I swirled my snifter, took a sip, and realized that I was in trouble. I told Judy "we have to leave now," said our goodbyes, and rode down the elevator that to me felt like a roller coaster. As Judy hailed a cab, I deposited my meal into a sewer drain on Central Park West. I was starting to have my doubts about the legal world.

I had started to look for a legal job for the summer, but jobs for first-year law students were hard to find. I had a couple of interviews and was waiting to hear back when my mother called. My father had another heart attack and was back in the hospital. I hung up the phone and sat on the edge of my bed and cried, but I'm not sure if I was crying for my father or for me or for both of us. Sloan Products beckoned again. My summer plans were made for me.

Just as I had after my first year of college, I spent the summer after my first year of law school taking over my father's sales route. I had use of a Sloan Products' car for the season, leaving Manhattan early each morning so I could be in Matawan by 8:00, then doing eight to ten hours of driving to see my father's customers before heading back to the city. I felt like there was an anvil on my chest, a dead weight that was holding me down against my will. Nothing was going according to plan.

Chapter Thirty-Three

It was around this time that my father's sister Ellie died, succumbing to a several years battle with brain cancer. Her mother, my Grandma Lena, was no longer living at my Aunt Ceil's, having been moved into a nursing home in Glen Cove on Long Island. Lena knew that Ellie had been sick, but my father, my Uncle Jerry, and my Aunt Ceil determined that Lena could not handle the knowledge of her daughter's death. They never told her.

Periodically, Judy and I would drive to Long Island with my parents to visit my grandmother at the nursing home. First, we would stop in Roslyn to pick up my Aunt Ceil. As soon as we entered Lena's room, she would start asking "How's Ellie?"

My father and Ceil looked at each other, than stared at their feet, before my father responded "Not good, Ma, not good."

"I never hear from her. Will someone please tell me what's going on?"

After more foot shuffling and uncomfortable glances, Ceil said "She's not doing so well, Mom."

I suffered through this farce on at least a dozen occasions. Finally, I could not take it anymore. I confronted my father in the nursing home parking lot.

"How can you keep doing this to Grandma? She has a right to know about Ellie. You think she hasn't figured it out? Well, I'm sure she has. All that you and Aunt Ceil and Uncle Jerry are doing is denying her the ability to mourn. It's sick."

"Watch how you to talk to me. She's old and frail. She couldn't handle it."

"Why don't you give her a little credit," I said as I walked away towards the car. What is it with my family, I asked myself. Are they all incapable of telling the truth, of letting people feel what they are supposed to feel? Sometimes I felt like pulling my hair out.

Chapter Thirty-Four

In September of 1976, when I was twenty-two, serendipity changed my life course. I had slogged my way through another summer at Sloan Products, and I was back at school, ready to focus on my life away from Matawan. As I started my second year at NYU Law School, I now needed a part-time job to supplement Judy's paralegal salary. I stopped by the law school's placement office. Tacked to the bulletin board outside the office, partially hidden by fliers announcing campus events, was an index card listing a law clerk opportunity at a small law firm of which I had never heard, Lipper Lowey & Dannenberg. I called the contact person, a young lawyer at the firm named Doug MacKay, and arranged an interview for the next day. It turned out that like me, Doug had attended Columbia, and he hired me on the spot without discussing it with the partners of the firm. On September 13, 1976, I walked through the doors of Lowey Dannenberg for my first day of work. A month later, Doug left the firm to start his own practice, and even though I was only a second year law student, I suddenly became the firm's de facto and sole associate, researching, writing, photocopying, serving and filing my own briefs.

Lowey Dannenberg was a litigation firm, primarily handling cases on behalf of large groups of investors who had been defrauded. At the time I started working at the firm, there were four attorneys and me, yet we were litigating cases against the largest law firms in the country. The David versus Goliath nature of the practice appealed to me, and I saw an opportunity to do some social good and make a nice living at the same time. More important to me, however, was the way the firm's partners allowed me to do my work in my own style. They did not try to mold me into an aggressive, attack dog type of litigator. They appreciated my scholarly, disciplined, and organized approach. That partially hidden index card on the placement office bulletin board had led me to a practice for which I was especially suited. I still had strong misgivings about whether I wanted to be a lawyer, but if I was going to practice law, I had at least found a place where I could be myself.

The firm was run by a mercurial lawyer named Dick Dannenberg. His mind worked faster than anyone I had ever met (I referred to him as a human supercomputer), but he also had a volatile personality, capable of detonating into a screaming fit at any moment. He became my mentor. My years of working for Olga had prepared me well for dealing with histrionics, but unlike Olga, Dick's tirades could not hide his heart of gold and his astonishing generosity. The joke in the office was that it was worth being on the receiving end of one of Dick's rants because he would then give you a raise the next day. Yet, he never raised his voice to me. More than anyone I ever knew, Dick appreciated my talents and praised and encouraged me constantly.

Lowey Dannenberg became the source of my true legal education. I was soon working there 20-25 hours a week, and my classes at NYU became a necessary but unfulfilling drudgery. Unlike my denim-clad classmates, I now wore suits to class, racing out the door as soon as I was done for the day so I could get uptown to the office where the real legal world awaited.

With my schedule and work load, and Judy's continued responsibilities at S&C, another academic year passed with minimal contact between us. We rarely had time for the academic debates we had engaged in while in college. Instead, Judy would periodically try to goad me into arguments about what I felt were petty distractions, usually her feelings about what she perceived as my family's unwarranted intrusions into our life. Between school and my job, I had enough on my mind. I refused to engage, which drove Judy crazy.

That year, Judy decided to go to law school. In the spring of 1977, she was accepted to NYU. The following academic year, we would both be in school (although I would still have my part-time job at Lowey Dannenberg). We needed to reduce our expenses, so we moved from Greenwich Village to a much cheaper apartment in a brownstone in Brooklyn Heights, a fifteen minute subway ride to NYU law. Judy was going to leave S&C at the beginning of August, and I was going to work as a summer associate at Lowey Dannenberg for the months of June and

180

July. I had been asked to be a bridegroom at a Steve Krasner's wedding in San Diego in August, and Judy and I figured this might be our only chance to drive cross-country. It would be a four-week trip, getting us back in time for classes in September.

I had one exam left before I was finished for the academic year, Trusts and Estates at 9:00 on a Friday morning in mid-May. At 3:00 that morning, our phone rang. I struggled to pick up the receiver.

"Hello," I mumbled.

"Neil, its Linda," Judy's sister said. "My father had a heart attack and died a little while ago."

"Oh shit. Hold on, I'll get Judy."

I leaned over and roused Judy. "Linda is on the phone. Your father died."

Judy sat on the edge of the bed, rocking back and forth and crying as she talked to her sister. When she hung up, she did not say a word to me. She dialed a number, calling her friend Barbara Zipperman, another paralegal at S&C. Judy wailed as she told Barbara what had happened. I sat there trying to comprehend why my wife would seek comfort from a friend when her husband was sitting right next to her.

Judy took the first flight to Boston that morning. I took my exam and followed later that afternoon. My parents came to Haverhill for the funeral. In the weeks that followed, Judy remained detached, obviously focused on her loss and her mother's new situation. There were several trips to Haverhill that summer.

When we were in New York, it was brutally hot. It was the summer of the Son of Sam and the big blackout. When the power went out, we were sitting in our Brooklyn apartment, trying to stay cool in the sultry summer heat. Within an hour or two, the looting began. Our apartment was about a five minute walk from the commercial district of downtown Brooklyn, and we could hear the sounds of breaking glass and police sirens all night long. After Judy's father died, we had debated whether we should cancel our cross-country trip, but getting out of New York now seemed like a good idea.

Chapter Thirty-Five

I reveled in the planning of our extended vacation. Our dining table became my base of operation, with tour books and maps spread all about. It was as if I had returned to the days when I got lost in my World Book, reading about far away places and adding layers of information to my already expansive knowledge of geography. I created a detailed itinerary, charting our driving routes, reserving inexpensive motel rooms, contacting people we could stay with in some of the places we were going to visit, and plotting our activities along the way. While I was working at Lowey Dannenberg that summer, I daydreamed often about the trip, re-working my plan in my head over and over.

Our mode of transportation was a light blue 1974 Buick Apollo, courtesy of Sloan Products, a loan arranged by my mother. The night before our departure, she called me.

"I don't want you to go to Yellowstone."

"Why not?"

"I just spoke to one of my college friends, and she told me that the son of someone she knows was murdered while he was sleeping in his tent there."

"First of all, we won't be camping. Second, if we ruled out every place in the country where there has been a murder, we would have to cancel the whole trip. Don't worry, we'll be fine."

We left as planned the next day on our grand circle of the United States: New York to Denver in two days, where we stayed with Howie and Marilyn for a few days in their new house, part of our program to repair that relationship; after some day trips in the Rockies, it was north to Wyoming and the national parks of Yellowstone and Grand Teton. We then veered southwest, driving across a sliver of Idaho, and were on the road in Logan, Utah when the meltdown hit.

I was driving and Judy was in charge of the maps. Somehow we lost the highway and ended up in a Logan sub-division. That's when the screaming started.

"What are you doing?" Judy yelled. "We're supposed to be on I-15."

"No shit," I screamed back. "You've got the map. It's your job to tell me where to go."

"Get us out of here now."

It went downhill from there. It was as if the tension of the last few months—the death of Judy's father, dealing with her mother, the heat in New York, our jobs, Judy stopping work to start law school in the fall—boiled over on a quiet suburban Utah street. We were shouting at the top of our lungs, making little sense. As we were going at it, I flashed back to the night in May when Judy's father died, and how she chose to call a friend rather than reach out to me. Something was not right.

Our storm blew over, and we found our way back to the highway and then on to Salt Lake City, acting as if nothing had happened. Our travels continued across the desert to Lake Tahoe, followed by San Francisco, Monterey, Big Sur, Los Angeles, and Krasner's wedding in San Diego. From California we drove to Las Vegas, the Grand Canyon, and across Arizona and New Mexico. When we stopped for the night in Albuquerque, we had three days to get back to New York. We drove for brutally long stretches as we pushed the Apollo to its limits, stopping only for gas, food, and a little sleep when absolutely necessary. We made it, and when I finished carrying our bags up to our third floor Brooklyn apartment and collapsed on the bed, I felt like my body was still moving at seventy miles per hour.

I called my mother to let her know we were back. "We just walked into the apartment, Mom. Back without a scratch."

"Honey, remember when I told you about that murder in Yellowstone. Well, I was wrong. It was in southern Utah. It's a good thing you didn't change your plans."

In many ways, the trip was everything I had envisioned. I fell in love with the grandeur of the west, places that I would visit again many times. I did my first hiking in the mountains, saw moose and bear, and sat on the banks of a river in Yellowstone as a geyser arced across the water while an elk grazed beneath the spray. I visited Disneyland, a place I dreamed about as a young boy watching "The Wonderful World of Color" on Sunday nights. And we did it all under our budget, even pulling out of gas stations without filling up because we were outraged by the seventy cents a gallon they were charging for gas. But the intensity of Judy's anger as she screamed at me on that street in Logan, Utah was something I carried with me, too.

Chapter Thirty-Six

The 1977-78 academic year, my last year in law school and Judy's first, zoomed along. I worked even more hours at Lowey Dannenberg and accepted their offer of full-time employment. I would start in August 1978, after I took the New York bar exam. Judy was buried under the workload of a first-year law student. I helped out when I could. On an October evening in 1977, I sat in front of our TV, typing a law school paper for her as she handed me handwritten sheet after handwritten sheet, while I watched Reggie Jackson bring the world championship back to Yankee Stadium with three home runs.

I had completely disappeared off of Olga's radar by then. Sandi was pregnant, due to give birth to Olga's first great-grandchild in March or April, and Eddie was marrying his college sweetheart, Linda Kames, in June. Olga was pre-occupied with these events, and did not seem to notice that I was about to finish law school with no intention of coming back to Sloan Products.

We also made new friends that year. A newly married couple, Josh and Jackie Weisberg, moved into the apartment two floors above us around the time we returned from our cross-country trip. Josh was a know-it-all like me, and we hit it off immediately. Given Judy's law school workload, I spent many hours two flights up.

On April 2, 1978, Sandi gave birth to Daniel Seth Edelstein. Olga, who for years had little use for Sandi's husband Howie, now adored the man who gave her a great-grandchild. Sandi and Howie had recently moved into a house in Old Bridge, New Jersey, a scant mile-and-a-half from 59 Freneau Avenue, and their proximity gave Olga a perfect excuse to be a daily presence in their lives. Danny became the new beneficiary of Olga's largesse, with the complete Sloan Products' baby toy inventory at his disposal. The four goonks and our four mates gathered in New Jersey after the birth to pose for a group portrait, Danny cradled in his mother's arms like royalty surrounded by his admirers.

In contrast, my graduation from law school barely created a ripple. My parents joined Judy at Town Hall for the ceremony, and that was about it. I immediately turned my attention to studying for the bar exam, taking a review class and cramming every waking minute, except for my daily break to run along the Brooklyn waterfront. I lost twenty pounds that summer, my weight back to the same 140 pounds I weighed when I was fifteen. Judy spent the summer working for the Legal Aid Society's Prisoner Rights' Project. For the first time in years, we spent next to no time in Matawan that summer.

I took a break from my studies for a weekend trip to Massachusetts for Eddie's wedding to Linda. Judy's mother was a guest, her first social affair since her husband's death the year before, and Judy focused most of her attention on her mom. The men in the wedding party, including me, were resplendent in our beige tuxedos and ruffled shirts, a poor Jewish excuse for a Motown singing group. My brother escorted Olga down the aisle, as she did a reprise of her act at Sandi's wedding, blowing kisses to the crowd.

Eddie made the mistake of telling me what room at our hotel that he and Linda were staying in that night, and when they finally left their guests for their wedding night, I stood outside their door making barnyard noises and cooing like a pigeon. My comrade-in-arms for all those years at Sloan Products, my childhood companion and mutual escapist, and keeper of so many of my deepest secrets, was now a married man. He and Linda would be returning to Denver, where they were both completing graduate school in psychology, and would then move to Los Angeles shortly after they graduated.

In late July, I took the two-day, grueling New York bar exam in the ball room of the Roosevelt Hotel in Manhattan. I thought I had done okay, until I overheard a conversation in the elevator following the last session of the test.

"Did you catch that doctrine of worthier title issue in the last essay question?"

"Sure did. They tried to sneak that one by us."

Not only had I not spotted the issue, I could not even remember what the hell the doctrine of worthier title was. I fretted for a minute, and then forgot about it. I had my job at Lowey Dannenberg waiting for me. But first, I had one last piece of unfinished business.

Chapter Thirty-Seven

When Howie, Sandi, and Eddie graduated college, Olga bought each of them a car at Straub Buick, the dealership in Keyport where she bought most of the vehicles for Sloan Products. When I graduated, I got nothing although I tried to convince myself that was merely because I was about to attend law school in New York City and had no particular need for a car. But three years later, wanting a car and still smarting from Olga's refusal to give us financial assistance when I started law school, I asked Olga if she would buy me one. She grudgingly agreed.

Olga wanted me to get a Buick, but I wanted a Japanese car. Owning a foreign car was like an act of heresy in our family, and I literally had to beg Olga to come with me to a Honda showroom. The car salesman ushered Olga and me into his office, a small room containing a battered metal desk, two vinyl covered guest chairs, and stacks of Honda brochures. A small window looked out to the showroom floor and the gleaming, new Japanese cars on display. With his red and black checked polyester sports jacket and carefully coiffed hair, the salesman looked like a game show host. At every step of the process, Olga tried to hondle with the Honda salesman, as she always had with Charlie Straub. But the Honda salesman patiently explained and re-explained that there was so much demand for Japanese cars that there were no discounts available— the price was the sticker price and not one cent less. She finally relented and agreed to a deal.

A few days later, my mother drove Olga and me to the Honda dealership to pick up my new car. Olga pulled her chair to the edge of the salesman's desk, put on the rhinestone studded glasses which always hung on a chain around her neck, and pored over the paper work. He said "All I need is the $5,000 balance and we're all set." Olga took out her wallet and removed a wad of $100 bills which she placed on the desk. The salesman counted the money. "There's only $4,900 here." I turned red with humiliation.

Olga turned her now empty wallet inside out, showing it to the salesman. "That's all I have. You'll just have to take it."

"Lady, I've explained this to you over and over. The sticker price is the price. Unless I get another $100, there is no sale."

Olga looked at the salesman with a cold-blooded stare, her face turning crimson. After several seconds, she reached into her purse and pulled out a little pink plastic rain bonnet container. She opened it and carefully removed a $100 bill, folded to the size of a small coin. She slowly unfolded it, smoothed the creases, and slammed it on the desk. "I hope you choke on it," she said.

As I sat there and watched Olga's performance, I thought to myself "It's not worth it. I'm never asking her for anything again." And I never did.

The salesman handed me the keys and took me out to the lot, where he reviewed the features of my new gold Honda hatchback. I slid into the driver's seat, adjusted the mirror, and slipped a cassette of "Born to Run" into the tape player. I pulled onto the Garden State Parkway as Springsteen implored "so roll down the window and let the wind blow back your hair." I followed his advice, leaving New Jersey and Sloan Products behind me. Soon I would be back in New York City, where my new career was waiting.

Part V

So This Is How It Ends

Chapter Thirty-Eight

In August 1978, I started my full-time legal career at Lowry Dannenberg. My responsibilities were no different from what I had been doing the previous two years; there was just more of it. I threw myself into my work, channeling my self-discipline as I had when I was methodically working my way through the encyclopedia when I was ten, or when I was exploring the world of books as a teenager, or reading every page of every assigned text as a Columbia student. My employers soon realized that I could handle anything they threw at me. My assignments grew exponentially. So did my hours. I was in the office many nights a week, and often on the weekend, too.

Judy's schedule matched mine. She was in her second year at NYU Law, working part-time at Legal Aid, and on the staff of The Commentator, the NYU Law school newspaper.

That Thanksgiving, we traveled to Haverhill to celebrate with Judy's family, our first road trip in my new Honda. Even though we were not spending the holiday with my family, Olga's presence still permeated our drive as I zipped along in the car she reluctantly bought me. And I could not help noticing the contrast as we gathered for the holiday meal in Judy's parents' house: unlike the Thanksgivings of my childhood, everyone sat together and there was no arguing.

When we returned to Brooklyn at the end of the long weekend, I pulled the car in front of our building, dropped off Judy and our bags, and went looking for a place to park. Ten minutes later when I bounded up the steps to the brownstone, Judy was standing in the vestibule holding a white business envelope. She handed it to me without a word, and I saw it was from the New York State Bar Examiner's office. My hands shook as I tore it open. I only had to read as far as the opening "Congratulations" to realize that I had passed. Judy and I embraced, my hand still tightly clasped around the letter.

My journey from Sloan Products' apprentice to licensed professional was complete.

With my license to practice law came more responsibility. I was soon appearing in court and taking depositions. And traveling. Lowey Dannenberg handled cases across the country, and I became the firm's main road warrior. At times, it seemed home was merely a place to change my clothes.

I started to make some decent money, too. Although I spent little time in our apartment, Judy and I agreed in early 1979 that it made sense to buy a place rather than to keep paying rent. So whenever we had a free Saturday, we looked at co-ops and brownstones in Park Slope, a historic brownstone neighborhood in the midst of rapid gentrification. The Slope was further into Brooklyn than where we were living, bordering the west side of Prospect Park. I fell in love with the neighborhood, but it soon became apparent that the Slope was out of our price range. I did not feel that I could ask my parents for advice about the process since they never owned a place of their own, yet another item in the list of my father's disappointments. When our broker asked if we would be willing to look at a house on the other side of the park, we immediately agreed.

The house was located on a small cul-de-sac called Albemarle Terrace, a row of brick Georgian townhouses with dormer windows and black shutters, built in 1916 behind the Dutch Reformed Church of Flatbush. The street seemed like it belonged in London instead of the heart of Brooklyn. Albemarle Terrace, and the adjacent cul-de-sac of Kenmore Terrace, was a small enclave populated by older couples and young Yuppie families in the midst of a Brooklyn neighborhood that was predominantly West Indian. It was a five minute walk from the south end of Prospect Park. We bought the modestly priced house at 2107 Albemarle Terrace and moved in shortly after Judy finished her second year of law school. My parents did not care for the neighborhood, but my father took pride in my home ownership, something he had never accomplished. I do not recall Olga ever setting foot in that house.

A few months later, when the house on Kenmore Terrace immediately behind ours became available, we convinced our friends and former upstairs neighbors Josh and Jackie to buy it. Our backyards bordered each other. We were like the Ricardo and Mertz families on "I Love Lucy," constantly walking in and out of each other's houses. Josh, Jackie, and I commuted to work together each morning, driving into Manhattan in Josh's red Mazda as we listened to Steve Post's liberal talk radio show on WBAI.

Judy and I spent our free time that summer working on our house. There was the paint-stripping project in the kitchen that we never completed. We removed wall-to-wall carpeting until our knees ached, and then hired someone to re-finish the wooden floors. Judy planted bulbs in our flower beds and impatiens in the window boxes. Then when the original 1916 toilet on the third floor started to run incessantly, I decided to fix it myself.

I went to Sears and bought a new flush lever, flapper valve, and float. There was no shut-off valve on the third floor, so I went down to the basement and shut-off the main water valve to the house. I removed the old inner workings of the toilet, and closely followed the instructions as I installed the replacement parts. An hour later, I was ready for a test run.

"Judy, go down to the basement," I said "and turn the water back on. I'll either yell 'okay' or 'turn it off' depending what happens."

When Judy opened the valve, a geyser erupted from the back of the toilet. As I screamed "Turn it off! Turn it off!" an expanding pool of water formed on the bathroom floor, water trickling down the hallway of the second floor, running down the pale yellow walls of our first-floor living room. I had created a three-story flood. By the time I arrived in the living room, Judy was already there, staring in disbelief at our newly stained wall. She did not say a word, and as she turned to look at me her expression did not change.

As I looked over the dismal results of my handiwork, I realized that in all the years that I lived at 59 Freneau Avenue, no one had showed me how to fix anything. The best thing I could do with my law degree was hire people to fix things for me. When the plumber arrived later that day, he looked into our toilet and said "Who's the idiot that did this?"

Although Judy and I were doing the things that young homeowners do together, we were still spending large amounts of time apart. I was working long hours or out of town. She spent much of her free time with the other staff members of The Commentator, who were often coming and going from our house. And as I spent more of my work day asking questions to witnesses, I had less and less inclination to ask questions at home. Rarely did I probe Judy about what was on her mind. I was my oblivious self, still lost in my own private world.

Later that year, as part of a routine examination, Judy was diagnosed with endometriosis, a condition in which endometrial cells are deposited in areas outside the uterine cavity. The condition often became an impediment to fertility. Her gynecologist suggested that if we were contemplating starting a family, the sooner the better. We talked about it that night.

"Given what the doctor said, I think I should try and get pregnant."

"I don't know. I'm still so early in my career, we just bought the house, and you're not even finished with law school. And what about your career?"

"If the timing works out, I could have a baby after I graduate, maybe right after the bar exam. I could then take a few months off before I start working full-time. Don't worry about your career. They love you. Plus I'll be taking more of the responsibility with the baby."

"I have to think about it."

But I didn't think about it. I didn't ask Judy any more questions. I gave it about as much thought as my decision to apply to law school. And I knew on some level that it wasn't worth battling Judy. Her resolve was greater than mine; she would wear me down eventually, so why not capitulate? I wanted my own family anyway, so what was the big deal if it was a little sooner than I had planned? We started our pregnancy efforts.

Judy and I proceeded with our plans. By the late fall of 1979, she was pregnant.

Chapter Thirty-Nine

Judy's pregnancy progressed. She was due in early to mid-August of 1980, and so was one of her law school classmates, Doris Traub. They compared notes constantly as they made plans to take the New York bar exam together in the end of July. As for me, work still dictated my schedule, but I approached fatherhood with nervous anticipation. I read Dr. Spock, attended Lamaze classes with Judy, and went with her on shopping trips to pick out wallpaper and buy furnishings for the nursery we were planning for the small room adjacent to our bedroom.

My parents were excited about our news, especially my father. He loved Sandi's son Danny, but the prospect of the first Selinger grandchild thrilled him. He began to dote on Judy. Olga, however, paid little attention to us. Judy's mother Molly, a chronic worrier, started a nightly ritual of calling us before she went to bed to make sure Judy was all right.

While we were preparing for parenthood, my brother and Marilyn continued to deal with their own medical issues regarding pregnancy. They had been trying with no luck, and Marilyn was finally directed to a fertility expert from Scandinavia who was working as a visiting physician at a hospital in Brooklyn not far from our house. Howie and Marilyn came to New York, and while Marilyn was in the hospital for a procedure, her sister Sheila stayed with us. Within a matter of months, Marilyn was pregnant, too, due in December. My father was on cloud nine.

One Sunday that spring, my parents came to Brooklyn. They wanted to buy a crib and a stroller for their new grandchild, so the four of us went to a large baby supplies store in the largely Orthodox Jewish neighborhood of Borough Park. We made our purchases—a crib that could convert into a youth bed and a bright red Perego stroller—and returned to our house. Before they left to drive back to New Jersey, my father went upstairs to use the bathroom. As soon as they left, I went up there, too. I walked in the door and turned on the light. Sitting on the edge of the sink was a large rat.

I screamed, a guttural "Aaaah!" which I barely recognized as my own voice. The next thing I knew I was flying back down the stairs and was practically hyperventilating when I found Judy.

"There's, there's a big rat in the bathroom. It must have been in there when my father was pissing."

"We need to go back up and find out where it is," Judy said calmly.

"No way. Let's call an exterminator."

Judy started climbing the stairs. I went to the basement and grabbed a shovel before I found her walking out of the bathroom.

"It's not in the bathroom, but there are droppings in there. Let's check the other rooms."

We tiptoed into the spare bedroom, where we saw the rat cowering in the corner. I probably scared it as much as it had scared me. We shut the door and filled the crevice between the door and tread with rolled-up towels.

I called an exterminator. He came in about an hour and slid a large trap into the bedroom, and then he put poison around the basement where he secured an open drain that was the rat's likely entryway into the house. The exterminator said he would return in the morning.

Then we waited.

In the middle of the night, we heard a loud snap. When the exterminator arrived, Judy and I stood behind him as he slowly opened the bedroom door. I had my trusty shovel in my hand. The trap had got him; the rat was stiff.

"Would one of you please get rid of it?" Judy asked.

Neither the exterminator nor I moved. "I hate this part of the business," he said. "Rats give me the creeps."

"So what are you saying, that you like roaches?" I asked him, still not moving.

196

Judy looked at the two of us with disdain. So my pregnant wife calmly walked to where the rat was laying, picked up the trap and its victim, and went outside and deposited it in a trash can. When she came back in and looked at me again, her expression had not changed.

Judy made it through her remaining weeks of law school. She spent the summer preparing for the bar exam. It was another hot summer in New York. The only air conditioner in our house was in our bedroom, so I moved a desk in there so Judy could study in comfort. On the day of the exam, I drove Judy and her classmate Doris to the exam site at the Grand Hyatt in Manhattan. I escorted them into the hotel, a waddling, extremely pregnant woman on either side of me. People passing me on the street gave me looks that said "What a man!"

Doris gave birth to a daughter a few days after the exam. Weeks passed, and Judy was now overdue. I moved a sewing machine into our air conditioned bedroom, and Judy made curtains for the nursery while she waited.

At the end of August, Howie and Marilyn came east to visit my family. On August 28, they had lunch with Judy in the city, and then the three of them came to my midtown office. Judy and Marilyn posed for pictures belly to belly in front of our law book laden shelves. That night, Judy went into labor. We were standing on our front step, getting ready to go to Lenox Hill Hospital in Manhattan, when the phone started ringing.

"That's your mother," I said. "Should I answer it?"

"No. We need to go."

I drove into the city like a madman. Judy, who never spoke softly, kept whispering "Could you try and avoid the bumps?"

Her labor lasted all night. Judy's mother kept calling our house every fifteen minutes. She tried the hospital, too, but she could not remember my last name and was therefore unable to get any information. In the middle of the morning of August 29, 1980, Hannah Lee Selinger, named after my grandfather Harry Selinger, arrived. I held her in the delivery room, and then went and watched her through the nursery window before I started making all my phone calls. She was sucking her two middle fingers. I could not take my eyes off of her. For the first time in my life, I felt like there was something in the world that I could truly call my own.

Chapter Forty

In the weeks and months following Hannah's birth, I thought we were a happy family. To me, it felt like things were never better. My father was happier than I had ever seen him, too. His granddaughter gave him great joy. I did not want to deny him this gift, so we starting spending more time in Matawan on the weekends. I did not realize at the time that each of these visits was driving a wedge between Judy and me.

On December 5, 1980, Marilyn gave birth to my nephew, Gil Bennett Selinger. We planned a trip west for the holidays, a few days in Los Angeles to see Eddie and Linda, and then on to Denver to visit Howie, Marilyn, and their new baby. On a frigid Christmas morning, Josh drove the three of us to JFK airport. When we arrived in L.A. it was 80 degrees. Hannah discovered the joy of her bare legs.

While we were in Denver, we soon discovered that none of us adults could distinguish Hannah's cries from Gil's. The four of us stumbled bleary-eyed down the upstairs hallway in the middle of the night as we tried to figure out which baby was awake. We spent New Year's Eve at a party at the home of friends of Howie and Marilyn, where Hannah and Gil slept side-by-side on a king sized bed, two peanuts surrounded by the barrier of pillows we placed around them.

By the time we got back to Brooklyn, we were exhausted. It was not long before the battles began. Not between Judy and me, but between Judy and Hannah. We were discovering that Hannah had inherited her mother's stubbornness and resolve. Neither would give an inch. They were the embodiment of the irresistible force and the immovable object. Judy was now working, a full-time Legal Aid lawyer, and whatever patience she had exhibited during Hannah's first months was wearing thin.

We hired a young woman from Grenada named Mary to take care of Hannah while we were at work. Hannah started talking early on, and there was a West Indian lilt to many of her phrases. Our streaked kitchen cabinets now contained salt cod and tins of sardines. Between our work schedules and exhaustion, Judy and I became the proverbial two ships that passed in the night. But I still insisted on regular visits to Matawan.

We also visited Haverhill. Over Columbus Day weekend, we picked up Judy's mother and the four of us drove to the White Mountains in New Hampshire. It was peak foliage season and we stopped at many of the scenic overlooks, Hannah nestled in a baby carrier on my back. It was the first time in a long while that we were together as a family unit away from our hectic daily work lives or the frenzy of 59 Freneau Avenue. I thought we were happier than ever.

Later that fall, we sold the Honda that Olga had reluctantly bought me. Getting an infant in and out of a car seat in the back of a two-door hatchback was wreaking havoc on our backs. We took the money we received in the sale and bought a small four-door Mazda with a manual transmission. I did not know how to drive a stick. The plan was for Judy to teach me, but we had trouble coordinating our schedules for the lessons.

That Thanksgiving, the three of us flew with my parents to Denver to spend the holiday weekend at my brother's. Judy was detached and remote the entire visit. She hardly spoke on the flight home.

Chapter Forty-One

A few weeks after we returned from Denver, Judy and I went to the movies to see "Reds."

As Warren Beatty and Diane Keaton found each other and embraced on the frigid Russian train platform, I reached over and took Judy's hand. She pushed my hand away, and as I turned to look at her in the darkened theater, I saw that she was crying. Then I saw anger in her eyes.

When the lights came on, we put on our coats. I tried to gauge Judy's mood, looking for any sign of what was troubling her. She would not make eye contact with me as she walked up the aisle with her head lowered. We stepped into the cold winter night air and walked across the parking lot towards our car. I took her gloved hand into mine, but again she pushed it away.

"I can't do this anymore," she said softly, staring at her feet.

"Can't do what?"

"This. Us."

"I have no idea what you're talking about."

"I can't be with you anymore. I don't want you to touch me anymore. Whenever I look at you, whenever you touch me, all I see or feel is your father. Do you get it?" She was yelling now. "You're just like your father. Weak. Self-pitying. Afraid to stand up to your family. He disgusts me. You disgust me." She ran to the car, leaving me standing there.

The air had been sucked out of me. She had never said any of this to me before.

I soon realized that I was still standing in the middle of the movie parking lot, shivering from the cold. I slowly found my way to the car and slid into the driver's seat. Judy was staring straight ahead.

I re-played bits and pieces of the last few years to see if there was some clue that I had missed, some message I had ignored. I knew Judy did not care much for my family, but most of the time neither did I. And my father? He was the world's nicest guy, even if he did feel sorry for himself, sorry over how Olga had broken a hundred promises about his stake in Sloan Products. What did that have to do with me? Maybe this was just another of Judy's moments of high drama, her typical over-reaction to some meaningless incident.

"I want you to move out," she said.

"You know what I think? I think you're out of your fucking mind. You never talk to me about any of this, never suggest we have a problem or that there are things we need to work on. Just drop this on me. Do you mind telling me how long you've been thinking about this?"

"A few years."

"A few years. You mean you were feeling this way before we decided to have a baby and you never said a word? Are you crazy?"

"I thought having a baby would help, make me feel better about us. And when I got my diagnosis, that just sealed it for me. But it only got worse with your family doting over her all the time. So I think you should move out. I know a couple of people who have an extra bedroom in their apartment."

"How convenient that you have this all worked out. What about Hannah, do you have that all figured out, too?"

"I thought she should always be at the house, but you and I could split our time there. I can stay with friends the nights you're home with Hannah."

"And you thought I would just say 'okay' and that would be that? You really are a piece of work sometimes."

We sat in uncomfortable silence as I drove home.

202

For the next few days, weeks, months, I was in a fog. When we were together, we tiptoed around each other, always avoiding what we should be talking about. We mostly talked about Hannah, her schedule, where will she go to nursery school, who will relieve Mary after work. We slept back to back, avoiding contact.

We tried a few sessions with a couples counselor, but Judy, who was never at a loss for words, was unable to tell either the therapist or me what the core problem was. The counselor assigned us some intimacy exercises which we dutifully performed, but they were perfunctory and devoid of feeling. We stopped going to the sessions. Instead, we worked longer hours to avoid each other, sleepwalking through our free time like two dazed and wounded animals, yet always keeping a wary eye on the other.

Judy seemed intent on making me miserable enough to give in, to just walk away. She spent most nights at a friend's apartment, letting me know at the last minute, leaving Hannah's care to me. And then I learned that her "friend" was a male co-worker with whom she was sleeping. Game, set, match. Judy had won.

I arranged to see the apartment that Judy had mentioned. It was a three-bedroom unit at West End Avenue and 92nd Street on Manhattan's Upper West Side. The two women who lived there, friends of a Legal Aid lawyer with whom Judy worked, were looking for a third roommate. The bedroom that was available was about the size of the small single dorm room I occupied as a student at Columbia. It would be a perfect place to wallow in my misery. I agreed to move in at the beginning of April. The understanding was that I would still be spending large amounts of my time at the house in Brooklyn.

We needed to tell Josh and Jackie what was happening. We had them over for dinner. I kept moving my fork around my plate, not really eating and not saying much. I could not take it any longer.

"You may have noticed over the last few months that things have not been copasetic around here. We tried to work on it, but we've decided to separate." I glanced at my friends, who looked stunned. I had thought that the tension between Judy and me had been obvious, but I was wrong.

"Hannah will always be here in the house, and we'll alternate being with her. I've rented a room in an apartment in Manhattan where I'll stay when I'm not here. I need to get some things up there this weekend."

"I'll be around," Josh said. "I'll help you."

"It's not necessarily the end," Judy added. "Maybe with a little time and space we can work things out." She was dangling a carrot in front of me.

There may have been more conversation, but by that point I had drifted off into my thoughts. A few days later, Josh helped me move a few pieces of furniture and some clothes into 673 West End Avenue.

Maybe Judy was right. Maybe I was weak. As this new phase of my life began, I could barely summon up the strength to make it through the day. I spent much of my time thinking about incidents which I thought were inconsequential but which, perhaps, Judy saw as evidence of my inadequacies: getting locked in her relatives' bathroom, knocking over Mrs. Engelman's vase, failing to convince Olga to lend us money for our apartment, not showing up for our rendezvous at the hotel in Denver, losing my wedding ring, my plumbing misadventure, watching her dispose of the rat.

I spent my nights lying in bed in the dark in the apartment to which I had moved, listening to Springsteen's album "The River" on my Walkman over and over and over, until the lyrics of each song were seared on my brain, until I could not take it anymore, trying to understand how my wife became "just another stranger, waiting to be blown away."

Chapter Forty-Two

I could not bring myself to tell my family. For the next six
months, I did not utter a word about our separation. It was a farce. I
visited Matawan often with Hannah, always making some lame excuse
why Judy could not make it, deluding myself into believing that no one
would notice what was going on. I considered myself a failure, and to say
out loud what had happened would only confirm it. I thought back to the
letter my brother had sent me when Judy and I got engaged. I dreaded an
"I told you so."

When I was in Manhattan, my life consisted of two things:
working and running. Lowey Dannenberg became my main distraction. I
spent 14, 15, 16 hours a day at the office. In the morning, I dragged
myself out of bed and drained every ounce of energy out of my body as I
ran back and forth through Riverside Park, 6, 7, 8 miles at a time.

When I was in Brooklyn, my life revolved around Hannah,
reading to her, feeding her, buying her toys. We went on errands and little
shopping trips together. The Mazda that Judy and I had bought with the
Honda proceeds was at my disposal, but our driving lesson plan was
ditched once we separated. I was left to teach myself by trial and error,
lurching around Brooklyn, the car jerking as I tried to change gears, or
stalling out. I could not mask my frustration. Each time I strapped
Hannah into her car seat, she asked "Daddy, are you going to say shit,
shit, shit again?"

Once Hannah was in bed, I would visit with Josh and Jackie.
They observed a lot when I was not around—the pitched confrontations
between Judy and Hannah, the male visitors to the house—and they
shared it all with me. In their way, they were urging me to move on, but I
was not ready to let go. Judy and I tried another unsuccessful round of
counseling. There were a few dates, and even a trip or two, but she treated
me like a platonic friend at best. I tolerated it all by convincing myself that

I had to exhaust every possibility of saving our family unit. I only managed to delay the inevitable.

By the fall of 1982, I could no longer continue lying to my parents. I met them for dinner in Manhattan.

"I'm sure you've noticed that Judy has not been coming with me to Matawan. Well, things have not been good. We're separated. I stay in an apartment uptown when I'm not with Hannah. We've been working on things, but I don't think it's going to work out."

"Oh, honey," my mother said. "We could tell. You should have said something."

For some reason, my parents decided that a family vacation was just what I needed.

Chapter Forty-Three

In the winter of 1983, twelve of us traveled to Nassau: my parents; Olga (naturally); Hannah and me; Sandi, Howie Edelstein, Danny, and his sister Carly (born in June 1981); and Howie, Marilyn, and Gil (Marilyn was pregnant). It was the last trip I took with either my father or Olga.

When we arrived in Nassau, a mountain of our luggage tumbled onto the carousel. One suitcase was missing: Olga's. She had a fit in the airport, but the laid-back Bahamian staff paid it no mind. They assured her that the bag would show up "eventually, mon." Olga had nothing to wear, and she was hardly an easy size to fit. She spent the week in the few oversized flowered dresses my mother managed to find.

For a day or two, it was sunny and warm, but when the clouds and cool weather arrived, we were ill-prepared. We spent our time trying to occupy our gaggle of small children who had come equipped for a beach vacation. There were trips to playgrounds, horse and buggy rides, and lunch in a Bahamian Burger King, not exactly what we had envisioned. Olga spent much of her time ensconced in front of a slot machine in the hotel's casino.

If one of the goals of the trip was to make me feel better, it was woefully unsuccessful. As a single parent responsible for a two-and-a-half year-old, I never had a moment for myself, other than one evening with my brother at the craps table while Sandi stayed upstairs with the sleeping brood. The trip also triggered memories of childhood vacations that I would have preferred to remain dormant. More than anything else, I was reminded at every juncture that as the one whose marriage had failed, the parent on the trip without a spouse, I was the odd one out of the four goonks. For someone who spent his entire childhood struggling with feelings of differentiation from my peers, this was not a happy set of circumstances.

On the last day of our trip, Marilyn and I were sitting in the lobby with our kids while my father and Olga were at the front desk checking out. The lobby had floor to ceiling windows, in front of which was a small ledge about four inches wide. Hannah was walking along the ledge like a tightrope artist when she lost her balance and fell into the space between the ledge and the window, where she disappeared from our view. Marilyn and I both screamed as we raced over, thinking that Hannah had plummeted to a lower level. All I could think about was how will I ever be able to explain this to Judy? When we got to the window, we looked down into a space only about a foot deep. Hannah was sitting there laughing. I grabbed her and hugged her so hard she wriggled to get free.

By the time I got back to New York, I was fuming. Angry at Judy for putting me in this position, angry at myself for not picking up on the many signals that Judy had been sending for years, angry that I was not like the rest of my family, angry that I was too much like my father. I had had enough.

Chapter Forty-Four

I told Judy that I was through with our arrangement of splitting time in the house in Brooklyn. I would visit Hannah there one or two nights a week, but Judy needed to come home after Hannah was asleep, and I would return to my apartment. On the weekends that Hannah was with me, she would stay with me in Manhattan (I had the room—one of my roommates got married and moved out). And the foot dragging and talk of reconciliation was over. I wanted to start the paperwork for a divorce. For the first time in our relationship, Judy did not push back. She merely said "okay."

I thought that finality would curb my anger. I was wrong. I was pissed off at the world. When my father entered Mount Sinai hospital for a series of tests recommended by his cardiologist in New Jersey, I was ticked off about that, too. I went to visit him there one evening.

"Explain to me again why you're here, Dad."

"My doctor back home wanted to get some test results, but this hospital is better equipped to do it."

"What kind of tests? What are they looking for?"

"It's no big deal. He just wants more information to make sure he's prescribing the right combination of drugs." He was sitting on the edge of his bed in a hospital gown, looking like a little boy as he kicked his bare legs back and forth. "Don't worry, Ace. Where do things stand with Judy?"

"We've pretty much agreed to the terms. She's looking over the agreement one more time. Everything should be done by my birthday."

"Good. It's time for you to move on."

Something did not feel right to me. My father was holding back about something. It was only later that I learned that his doctor had recommended bypass surgery. My father was at Mount Sinai to see if he was a candidate for the procedure. It was determined that his heart was too far gone, that he would not be able to withstand the operation. The only person he told was his brother, my Uncle Jerry.

For my thirtieth birthday, I got an executed set of divorce papers. Judy got the house at 2107 Albemarle Terrace and the Mazda. I got joint custody of Hannah and the engagement ring I bought Judy over my parents' objections. And I got Josh and Jackie. They had moved from the house behind Judy's to a duplex in Park Slope. They were through with her, but they were my closest friends.

I was feeling like a one-armed juggler in those days. I was swamped at work, and doing a lot of traveling to Pikeville, Kentucky in the heart of Appalachian coal country. I was representing a group of investors who lost $25 million in a phony strip-mining operation. Being one of the few Jews in 1950's Matawan was nothing compared to being a Jewish lawyer from New York in soot-covered Pikeville, where bearded rednecks in overalls drove pick-up trucks with shotgun racks and Confederate flags up and down the town's main drag. When I was in New York, I still spent as much time as possible with Hannah. And in between it all, I was trying my hand at dating. Then Judy called.

"Andy and I are going to Martha's Vineyard for a few days in February. Do you think you could stay in Brooklyn with Hannah for a couple of days? She has nursery school that week, so your apartment won't work. And Mary will be here to meet the bus when she comes home."

Sure. Walk all over me, what the fuck do I care? That's what I wanted to say. What came out of my mouth was "Why not?"

February 17-22, 1984, 2107 Albemarle Terrace, Brooklyn, NY and 59 Freneau Avenue, Matawan, NJ

I barely slept last night trying to grapple with the news about my father's death. I kept thinking about the frustrations that he let consume him and the insufferable role that Olga played in his life. At some point I dozed off, and when I woke up this morning it took me a few minutes to remind myself that I had not dreamt the whole thing.

After I hung up with my mother last night, I called our babysitter Mary to let her know what was happening. I then tried to reach Judy in Martha's Vineyard at the inn where she was staying. She was out, so I left a detailed message. This morning I still have not heard from her, but I do not have time to dwell on it. Mary just arrived and I have to get out to be with my mother.

When I arrive in Matawan, Olga is waiting at the top of the back stairs to the house. "It's horrible, horrible. He was such a good man. And your poor mother. Believe you me, I know what it means to lose a husband." I cannot bear to look at her. I walk past to find my mother, but first I see Sandi in the back hall. We hug, then I ask her "How did it happen?"

She tells me that my parents had gone to the city for the Toy Fair. Olga did not go with them. After they were done at the Toy Building, one of the sales reps took them out for dinner. "I guess they were having a nice time—I mean how often do they get to be in the city without Grandma?—and they lingered at the restaurant. Grandma was having conniptions, carrying on about how they must have been mugged or in a car accident. She was calling my house every five minutes to see if I had heard anything. When your parents got home, she went nuts, screaming at Uncle Jules, telling him he had some nerve making her worry like that, who does he think he is, that sort of thing."

"Her usual crap."

Apparently he got very upset about the whole thing. When Sandi saw him yesterday morning, he looked ashen. But he went on the road to see customers and a little after he got home he collapsed on the bedroom floor. He never regained consciousness.

"Did you come over last night?"

"I did. Grandma was in one of her 'woe is me' rants and I told her to just stop it, that she probably killed Uncle Jules by screaming at him. I can't believe I said that to her."

"Wow. Good for you. What did she say?"

"Nothing. She walked away."

I am still trying to picture the scene of Sandi finally standing up to Olga when my mother emerges from her bedroom. Her eyes are red and she looks tired. I hug her and kiss her on the cheek, but I have no idea what to say. All I can come up with is "Are you all right?"

"I'm sad, honey, but I'll be okay."

That is about all we have to say to each other. I escort my mother in silence to Bedle Funeral Home in Keyport. The funeral director presents a list of all the decisions we have to make: what type of coffin, burial shroud or suit, do we want them to remove his wedding ring. We make our selections. He hands my mother a small plastic bag containing my father's watch and some other personal belongings he had on him when he died. We drive home without saying a word.

By the time we get back to the house, Howie and Marilyn are there. They had flown all night and they look spent. Howie and I embrace. Eddie is on his way from California. The four goonks will be re-united for the first time in years.

We spend the day making calls to relatives and my parents' friends and finalizing the plans for the funeral and shiva. For once, the entire family eats dinner together. Marilyn looks at me from across the table and says "You should have Hannah here with you. Let's drive to Brooklyn and get her." I call Mary to let her know we are coming. She and Hannah are waiting for us when we pull up in front of the house in Brooklyn as Marilyn struggles to stay awake. Hannah wriggles free from Mary's lap, runs to me, and jumps into my arms. She is sucking the middle

212

and ring fingers of her right hand, the way she always does when she is tired or anxious. She removes them for a moment, says "Hi Daddy," then puts them back in her mouth as she rests her head on my shoulder.

"Mary, have you heard from Judy?"

"Not a word."

I am exhausted by the time we get back to Matawan, but I cannot sleep. Instead I sit at the dinette table where my father always sat in the morning reading the paper, and write a eulogy.

Temple Shalom, the congregation in Matawan my parents joined when they left Beth Mordecai, is packed for the funeral. Howie and I are to speak; my mother sits in the front row before us, dabbing the corners of her eyes with a tissue. Howie talks about what our father meant to him. I talk about what his family meant to my father. It takes all my willpower to hold back my tears, but when I see Jackie as I am walking to the limousine I collapse in her arms, sobbing uncontrollably.

As we sit shiva at my family's house for the next few days, hordes of people come and go. Mounds of food are constantly being delivered— deli platters, fruit baskets, cookies and cakes. The four goonks sit together, and we even manage to laugh. Hannah takes up residence in my lap. When visitors stop to admire her ringlets, she removes her fingers from her mouth for a minute or two and shows off her precocious vocabulary. Soon it is time to return to our lives.

I sit on the front stoop of 2107 Albemarle Terrace waiting for Judy to arrive. Hannah is upstairs, asleep. When the car pulls up, I walk right to the passenger door as Judy opens it.

"What's the matter?"

"Didn't you get my message? My father died."
"I never got it. I'm so sorry."

"Don't give me your bullshit. I figured you would be happy. It's what you wanted, isn't it? I mean, he disgusted you, right?"

I walk away before Judy has a chance to respond. On my way to the subway, I think about my father's life and my promise to him and myself that I would be my own man. It is time to make good on it. At so many points in my life, I vowed to move on, to leave the past behind. I am doing it again, but this time I will try and remember who I am and how I got here. It may take a while, but I think I am going to be okay.

I am, after all, a Sloan product.

Epilogue

I have a photo that hangs on the wall of my house that I look at almost every day. It was taken by my father's brother-in-law Manny Katz at a family Seder at 59 Freneau Avenue in 1948. Everyone looks so happy: Olga, her mother Becky, and Lena Selinger seated in the middle of the posed shot, large corsages pinned to their shoulders. Harry Selinger smiling in a way I do not recall ever seeing. Lined up in the back are Irving and Charlotte, Sadie and Annie, my parents, and my father's sister Ellie, all beaming as if they do not have a care in the world. Kneeling in front is Charlie, relatively thin and wearing a suit and tie. He has a big grin on his face. Next to him are my Uncle Jerry and his sister Ceil, still a teenager. I look at their faces, I recognize them, but I do not know who they are. What happened to this happy group? They do not exist in my memory.

No matter how many times I re-play the facts of my childhood in my head, I cannot figure it out. What was eating at Olga and Charlie that they had to fight every day? What was the hold that Olga had over her sisters and daughters that they agreed to live in her house for their entire lives? Why was my father so willing to put aside his aspirations in deference to my mother and her family? I am reconciled to the fact that I am never likely to know.

More puzzling is trying to comprehend the effect that life at Sloan Products had on Howie, Sandi, Eddie, and me. Notwithstanding every thing that went on around us—the screaming and cursing, the custody trial, the broken promises and unfulfilled dreams, not to mention the bad taste and over the top nature of the place—we all turned out okay. For the most part, we are thoughtful and considerate. We value hard work. We try to communicate with our spouses and our children. We are all in long-term relationships. Maybe living with and watching Olga taught us something, after all.

I broke away from the pull of Sloan Products, practicing law at Lowey Dannenberg for thirty-one years. I became a partner of the firm in 1984, only a few months after my father died. He never got to see the "& Selinger" that was added to the firm name. Over the course of my career, I argued cases and examined witnesses in seventy-five cities in thirty-four states and four Canadian provinces. At the end of 2007, I retired, leaving Lowey Dannenberg and my legal career behind. It was finally time to pursue the things that I thought I wanted when I left Matawan for Columbia, before that left turn into law school and the legal world.

Yes, Judy and I got divorced, and I ultimately took some responsibility for what happened to us. I was never fully present in our relationship. The traits I developed as a child to survive life at 59 Preneau Avenue—staying out of the fray, being an observer instead of a participant—did not serve me well during our marriage. Slowly and eventually, I became more engaged in the world around me, although I still drift off into space periodically. I have done a better job this time: my second wife Rima and I have been together for twenty-four years. She helped me find peace. Our daughters Emily and Julia joined Hannah to give me a trio of smart, wonderful, and beautiful girls.

The friends that saw me through many of my life's bumps are still there for me. My Northwood buddies Arnie Engelman and Dan Saltman remain good friends. Engelman is a theatrical producer in New York City, still living in Greenwich Village. Dan Saltman, a vaudevillian at heart—comedian, juggler, magician, who spent every waking moment entertaining us at camp-- is now a physician in Honolulu. Steve Krasner, who I met my first day at Columbia and was sports editor of our college newspaper, just retired after a long career as a columnist for the Providence Journal. We see each other regularly. Josh and Jackie have been my closest friends for over thirty years.

Howie still lives in Denver, where he is a clinical psychologist in private practice. He and Marilyn have been married for thirty-six years. Eddie now lives in Massachusetts. He and Linda have been married for thirty-two years; they are both psychologists, too. Sandi and Howie Edelstein are still married and living in New Jersey, thirty-seven years after Olga blew kisses to the crowd at their wedding. The four goonks are the

216

proud parents of nine children, all of whom call my mother Grandma Helen.

Olga died in 1986. Sadie, Annie, and Charlie all held on into their 90's. My mother was finally left alone in that big house that she had occupied since she was a young girl. With Sandi's help, she kept Sloan Products going until just a few years ago, but after sixty-five years in business the company was no longer economically viable. We convinced her it was time to close the doors.

The house and the property that my great-grandfather had bought in a tax sale during the depression were sold to a real estate developer, but the fifteen rear acres that Olga refused to sell for anything less than $15 million no longer had any commercial value—that part of the property was designated as protected wetlands and will remain green space forever. The house and the buildings of Sloan Products are all gone; a condo development has taken shape on the lawns we played on when we were the four goonks, and the street that runs through the complex is called Sloan Court. New Jersey's current economic bad times have not been kind to the project.

My mother now lives a few miles from 59 Freneau Avenue. At 84, she still exhibits the energy and indomitable spirit that defined her entire life. In the twenty-four years since Olga died, my mother has been free as a bird, coming and going as she pleases. She deserves that.

There was no doubt who was in charge of our Ponderosa—my grandmother Olda. Olga posing in front of her new business, late 1930s.

Front cover: Neil, age 8, on the deck of the S. S. Brasil, February, 1962.

Olga dressed in fur-trimmed silk and satin, somewhere in the wilds of Jersey, 1935.

The early days of Sloan Products.

Passover 1948, at 59 Freneau Avenue. Clockwise from bottom: Harry Selinger, Lena Selinger, Ceil Selinger, Ellie Selinger Katz, Annie Ungar, Sadie Ungar, Becky Ungar, Charlie Ungar, Olga Sloan, Charlotte Sloan Bauman, Irving Bauman, Helen Sloan, Jules Selinger and Jerry Selinger.

My parents' wedding portrait, May 1948.

One of the few pictures of Baby Neil and his parents and brother,
Fall 1953.

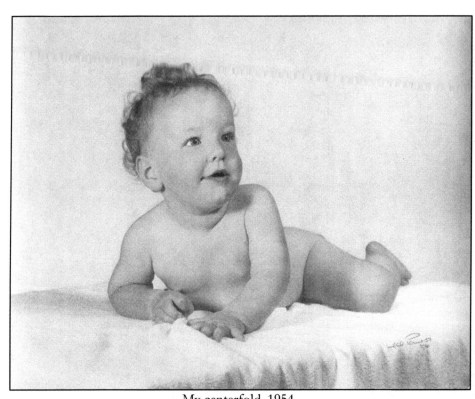

My centerfold, 1954.

"The Four Goonks" 1954; that's me on the left looking miserable, and Sandi, Howie and Baby Eddie on the right.

Posing in front of my father's DeSoto, 1956.

The Four Goonks, Halloween 1958, just a matter of days after Charlotte's death. That's me on the left, looking lost in space.

Just me and my shadow in my parents' living room.

The Selinger Family out on the town.

Standing in our back yard, 1961, with one of the old poultry farm sheds in the background.

Dinner on the S. S. Brasil, February 1962. Left to right: Olga, Sandi, Eddie, me, Howie, my mother and my father.

Annie, Charlie and Sadie coming off the ship after a Caribbean cruise.

My mother, newly blonde, posing like a movie star in the driveway of
59 Freneau Avenue.

Olga next to her prized possession, her Cadillac Sedan de Ville.

My parents and me following my Bar Mitzvah service, October 22, 1966.

Dancing with my mother at my Bar Mitzvah reception, October 23, 1966.

My family at my Bar Mitzvah reception. Left to right: Annie, Sandi, Olga, Eddie, my mother, me, my father, Howie, Sadie and Charlie.

Debbie Bernstein and me in the Camp Northwood production of
Oklahoma!, 1967.

Judy and me, young newlyweds, at Columbia University graduation, May 1975.

Baby Hannah on her Dad's back, Albemarle Terrace, Brooklyn, 1981.

The last picture of my father before he died, circa 1983.

The sign above the entrance to the office at Sloan Products.

Young lawyer returning home from work, Brooklyn 1978
(photo courtesy of Jackie Weisberg).

Back cover: Author's photo by Jackie Weisberg (www.jackieweisberg.com)

Acknowledgements

The list of people who helped me with this project is long. Thanks to my fellow writers at the Writing Institute at Sarah Lawrence College and the other members of the Bella Villa Writers group for their patience and insight over the last three years. Special thanks to my Zen writing guru Steve Lewis who helped me to stop writing like a lawyer and start writing like a human being. This book would not exist but for the tireless efforts of my agent Malka Margolies of the Salkind Literary Agency. A special thank you as well to my writing assistant Dr. Dana Gage, for her patience and encouragement. Thanks to Audrey Cozzarin of Solderelli Design for her loving restoration of the family photos that are included in this book.

To my friends who read my drafts and encouraged me throughout the process, I am eternally grateful. You are too numerous to mention here but I would be remiss in not acknowledging Josh and Jackie Weisberg for their careful reading and comments over the course of my work on the book, and for Jackie's permission to include her beautiful photos of me both young and old; I could not ask for two more devoted friends. And a special shout out to my fan club of Laura Chamberlain, Debbie Broder, and Diane Duckler. Your appreciation of my writing has helped sustain me.

This book is about my family and my family has rallied around me since I started working on it. To Howie, Sandi and Eddie I truly appreciate the time you spent scouring the details of my work and, for the most part, confirming my memories of life in Matawan. To my mother, I thank you for the fortitude it took to read my drafts and your understanding of my perspective about life at 59 Freneau Avenue.

My writer daughter, Hannah, helped me organize a disconnected group of anecdotes into something that resembled a draft of a book. I cannot thank her enough for her typing and editing skills. And thanks as well to my daughters Emily and Julia for taking the time to read and comment on my draft, even if it meant learning some of my deepest secrets; and for Emily's contributions as photo editor, sifting through hundreds of photographs.

Finally, thanks most of all to my wife Rima for her patience and understanding while I was preoccupied with this project. And thank you Rima for the beautiful covers that grace this volume.

Breinigsville, PA USA
16 January 2011
253393BV00001B/230/P